Understanding Family Policy

Understanding Family Policy

Theoretical Approaches

Shirley L. Zimmerman

SAGE PUBLICATIONS
The Publishers of Professional Social Science
Newbury Park   Beverly Hills   London   New Delhi

For information address:

SAGE Publications, Inc.
2111 West Hillcrest Drive
Newbury Park, California 91320

SAGE Publications Inc.
275 South Beverly Drive
Beverly Hills
California 90212

SAGE Publications Ltd.
28 Banner Street
London EC1Y 8QE
England

SAGE PUBLICATIONS India Pvt. Ltd.
M-32 Market
Greater Kailash I
New Delhi 110 048 India

Printed in the United States of America

Library of Congress Cataloging-in-Publication Data

Main entry under title:

Understanding family policy : theoretical approaches /
    Shirley L. Zimmerman.
        p.   cm.
    Bibliography: p.
    Includes index.
    ISBN 0-8039-2798-3   ISBN 0-8039-3226-X (pbk.)
    1. Family policy—United States.   2. Family policy.
I. Zimmerman, Shirley.
HQ536.U496 1988
362.8'2'.0973—dc 19   87-28597
                                            CIP

FIRST PRINTING 1988

Contents

PART IV   THE POTENTIAL OF FAMILY POLICY

Acknowledgments

This book was written out of the belief that the relationship between families and public policies at all levels and in all areas is important, and important to recognize and understand. The privacy rights of families, which are protected by the Constitution, have made it easy to deny or disregard this relationship both conceptually and practically. Not helping matters in this regard is the fact that related developments in the fields of family and policy studies have been independent of one another, feminist theory being an exception. This book attempts to link the micro and macro in ways that hopefully will be useful to those who would like a conceptual basis for understanding the relationship between families and public policies and its underlying influences; for influencing policy processes as they relate to families such that their outcomes are supportive of families; and those simply who may find this area of study to be as deeply and intrinsically interesting as I do.

The help, support, and goodwill that I received from friends and colleagues in this endeavor are gratefully acknowledged: Richard Hey who read and commented on the first draft of the book in its entirety; Edwin Shneidman who read and commented on selected chapters; Jan Hogan, Geraldine Gage, Pauline Boss, Paul Rosenblatt, and David Olson who encouraged my efforts and supported the way in which I conceptualized the book; the Family Study Center at the University of Minnesota, which is where I began my work in this area; the Agricultural Experiment Station and All University Council on Aging at the University of Minnesota, which funded some of the research reported in the book, as well as the Minnesota Developmental Disabilities Planning Program; the family representatives who participated in the various research studies; and research assistants Joyce Schultenover, Sherry Mulroony, Carol Eide, Jacquie Tascher, each of whom carried out phases of the different studies.

It is my family, however, that bore the real brunt of this undertaking. To them I say thank you for having done it so well and good-naturedly—

most of the time. Their names are: Peter, my spouse; Julie, Casey, Danny and Mike, our children; Lonnie, Irene, and Ellie, our three additional children; and finally, Rachel, Joel, Eli, and Joshua, our grandchildren.

Foreword

Dr. Shirley Zimmerman has drawn upon her vast experiences in family policy studies to provide an important guide to the development of family policy as it exists today and as it might be better developed tomorrow. In the book, Dr. Zimmerman has traced the development of public family values in light of our historical, philosophical, and cultural traditions, and developed a conceptual framework for analyzing these values and the impact of policy changes by drawing upon the disciplines of policy studies and family studies. In so doing, Dr. Zimmerman helps the reader to examine the effect of seemingly unrelated decision and policies upon families and our family values.

Our policymakers have begun to recognize that, for a variety of reasons, we have too long neglected the connection between policy choices and family outcomes. Through her insights in this book, Dr. Zimmerman helps to crystallize this recognition. It must be hoped that policymakers and public alike will take insight and understanding from her work, and realize that policy choices affecting families, even the choice to do nothing, are choices with critical consequences that can and must be carefully examined and weighed systematically as well as compassionately.

—Walter F. Mondale

PART I
LAYING THE FOUNDATION

CHAPTER *1*

Family Policy: Definitions, Domain, and Concepts

This book is about family policy. Although the United States does not have an overall, official, explicitly stated family policy, it is now widely recognized that almost all government policies affect families directly and indirectly, intentionally or not. The aim of this book is to provide ways for understanding policy as process and content and the family dimensions of policy. Because no one theoretical framework can encompass all family policy phenomena and because such phenomena can be understood in more than one way, a larger rather than smaller repertoire of such frameworks is required. Such frameworks are useful because they provide the concepts necessary for ordering and assigning meaning to observations of policy phenomena related to families, and vice versa, thus facilitating better understanding of them.

The policy perspectives that this book presents are drawn from the policy studies field; they include the rational and incremental choice frameworks, interest group, elite, and game theories. The family perspectives that this book presents, drawn from the family field include: conflict theory, symbolic interaction, exchange theory, family stress theory, and the systems framework, with special emphasis on the latter. To illustrate their usefulness, some of these frameworks will be applied in examining the relationship between families and policy.

Many of the frameworks overlap conceptually within and also between the family and policy fields. Such overlap should be advantageous to policy analysts and family specialists as they interface with one another around issues of common concern. By becoming familiar with the unique application of the frameworks to policy and families, family specialists will be better able to identify and understand the policy implications of their research and clinical work with families, and policy practitioners will be better able to identify and understand the family implications of their policy practice and research. The development of such common understandings portends both to improve the quality of family policy discourse, and to facilitate the development of policies that reflect better understandings of their family dimensions and implications. Those who work with policymakers, such as legislative staff, advocates, interest group spokepersons, school and health care personnel, social service workers in all kinds of settings and others just interested in families, have a special interpretive role to play in this regard.

To establish the terrain for the ensuing discussion, the remainder of this chapter will focus on definitions, of policy, social policy, and family policy, outlining their respective domains and highlighting their commonalities and distinctions.

Policy

DEFINITIONS, VALUES, AND ISSUES

According to Harold Lasswell (1968), policy focuses on fundamental and often neglected problems of individuals in relation to society. The term *policy* connotes choice with respect to the pursuit and achievement of goals or values. In contrast to topical issues, values persist and cut across topical issues that tend to wax and wane over time. Values pertain to individual freedom; family well-being; fairness, equity, or justice; equality of opportunity; life; rights; efficiency; economic security; quality of life; and so forth. Issues such as abortion, comparable worth and ERA, tax reform, deinstitutionalization, welfare reform, catastrophic health insurance, surrogate parenthood, teen pregnancy, homelessness, and jobs programs all involve values. Because all values related to specific issues cannot be pursued or achieved simultaneously, the political system has the task of ordering and ranking them in terms of their relative importance, and then of persuading society's members to accept its rankings as binding most of the time (Easton, 1968). Commitment to these rankings may be discerned by willingness to pay taxes, obeyance of laws, and general support of the aims of government under which individuals live.

Policy comprises a series of related choices or decisions to support an agreed upon course of action with respect to the pursuit and achievement of a goal or value, or as Kahn (1969) says, it consists of a cluster of overall decisions. The qualifier "agreed upon" course of action suggests that policy is a process of collective decision making governed by rules. Rules enable decision-making bodies to make choices, even when members are not in unanimous agreement about them. The rule or procedure that allows this is some version of majority rule. The extent of member agreement may be discerned from the distribution of votes on particular issues. A vote of 5 to 4 among members of a 9-member body indicates substantial disagreement among individual members with respect to that body's collective decision; a vote of 7 to 2 would indicate substantial agreement. Some decision-making bodies, such as Congress, have rules about rules, as illustrated by the rule that specifies whether an item can be on the legislative agenda for discussion and debate.

Because the problems that come to policymakers' attention cannot all be addressed at the same time and not all problems come to their attention, many may remain neglected for long periods. Also because of the values they hold, policymakers may not perceive certain phenomena, such as widening income disparities and homelessness, as problems. Such perceptions are not immutable, however, in that policymakers often are required to reorder their values in accordance with changes in the larger sociocultural-economic environment and to attend to phenomena they otherwise would disregard. Thus greater emphasis may be placed on the pursuit of efficiency and productivity at one point in time, as in the 1980s, while at another point in time greater emphasis may be placed on equality of opportunity and equity or fairness, as in the 1960s.

LEVELS AND SCOPE

As a term, policy can be used and applied to almost all levels of human endeavor: individual, family, group, organization, community, county, state, regional, national, and international—in public, quasi-public, and private sectors. Individuals, for example, may develop policies that guide their actions as illustrated by the individual who says, "It's against my policy" when asked to state his or her opinion about a political candidate or to reveal his or her party affiliation. Families similarly develop policies to guide their actions with respect to savings, for example, or expenditures for housing, vacations, or child rearing. Business and industry develop policies with respect to personnel, social concerns, and profit margins. Municipal governments develop policies concerning water, sewage, and noise control; parks and recreation;

libraries; and police and fire protection. School boards develop policies concerning the education of children and related matters. County governments develop policies with respect to income maintenance programs, and health and social services, including correctional and court services. State governments develop policies with respect to income maintenance programs, health and social services, employment and manpower programs, and natural resources. In terms of the federal government, it develops policies concerning defense and international affairs; general science, space, and technology; natural resources, the environment, and energy; aid to businesses, agriculture, and communities; human resources, such as education, employment and manpower, social services, health, income security, and veteran's benefits; law enforcement, justice, and general government; and general purpose financial assistance (U.S. Bureau of the Census, 1985).

Clearly, policies or decisions made at the federal level are the widest in scope in that they affect all citizens of the United States. In contrast, policies of lower levels of jurisdiction, such as states and counties, apply only to persons residing within them, although in some instances, they also apply to visitors—traffic and no smoking laws being examples. That state and county policies often are made to conform with federal policies and guidelines, as well as with each other, suggests that policymaking is highly interactive among the three levels of government. Reflecting not only compliance with federal law on the part of states and counties, state level policy also reflects the diffusion of policy responses to identified problems; one example being marital rape laws enacted in several states. Although policy applies to all levels of human endeavor, in both the public and private sectors, this book is mostly about decisions made by governments, not individuals and families, except as the latter has implications for the former, or serves to illuminate family/government relationships.

Social Policy

DEFINITIONS AND GOALS

Another term important to this discussion is *social policy*. If policy pertains to important choices with respect to an agreed upon course of action in the pursuit of a goal or value, what then is social policy? Baumheier and Schorr (1977) have defined social policy as consisting of principles and procedures that guide any course of action dealing with individuals and aggregate relationships in society. In so doing, their definition of social policy goes beyond Lasswell's to include problems of groups as well as individuals in relation to society. Conceiving of social policy as "intervention in and regulation of an otherwise random social system," they attempt to differentiate it from policy in other areas, such as the economy. However, because social policy also is concerned with the social consequences of policies in other areas, the separation of social policy from tax, defense, or farm policy—or foreign affairs, for that matter—is less clear than may first appear.

Emphasizing its social aspects, Baumheier and Schorr (1977) go on to say that social policy represents "a temporarily settled course of action with regard to selected social phenomena that govern social relationships and the distribution of resources within a society." Such action, according to Gil (1973), determines the nature of individual and group relationships within a society by regulating the development, allocation, and distribution of its statuses and roles and the entitlements that accompany them. Zoning laws that regulate the lot size and type of home construction for a given residential area, and consequently where families of different income levels may live, is an example of such regulation.

Kenneth Boulding's (1967) observations contrasting social policy and the free market are of interest in this regard. The latter, he said, is characterized by exchange in which "a quid is got for a quo," whereas the former is characterized by the transfer of goods and services based on some status, identity, or community that society has legitimized, such as low income or retirement age, or designated catchment area. The relational processes that are involved in transfers, he said, tend to foster social integration and discourage alienation, whereas those that are involved in market exchanges do the opposite. Such distinctions may no longer apply if indeed they ever did, as evidenced by public hospitals that refuse to admit persons who cannot pay for care, and others that require patients without insurance to make cash deposits before admission (Pear, 1985). The use of sliding fee scales and minimum service charges, now relatively common in social policy institutions in all sectors, public, voluntary, and nonprofit, also is indicative of the blurring of such distinctions.

According to Titmuss (1968) social policy acts to support the free market through government actions to meet a range of needs that the market does not or cannot satisfy for certain segments of the population. However, what constitutes need and the role that social policy should play in meeting it has been observed to change over time. Because social policy is concerned with needs that the market cannot or does not satisfy for certain segments of the population, it necessarily is concerned with issues of redistribution: vertically, in relation to individuals or groups in different income strata; horizontally, in relation to individuals sharing a similar status, such as mentally retarded and mentally ill persons; and longitudinally, in relation to parents and children and future generations.

The concept of social policy also extends to concerns about the social costs of economic production, such as lung disease resulting from air polluted by coal burning industries, physical impairment caused by industrial accidents, and psychological stress resulting from unemployment due to company mergers. Such costs are referred to as externalities—the production of goods or bads external to their calculated costs. Generally associated with that which is produced by private enterprise, social costs can arise as a consequence of public actions as well (Rein, 1976). Illustrative are the displacement of people and devaluation of property when highways are constructed through viable neighborhoods, and on a more devastating level, Three Mile Island. Social policy also is concerned with the distribution of social costs and the groups most affected by them—that is, with whether such costs are borne by some groups more than others, or those least able to bear them.

FUNCTIONS, SCOPE, AND PROVISIONS

According to Titmuss (1969), social policy, in manifesting the determination of society "to survive as an organic whole," performs a number of functions in addition to those associated with the free market. These include: (1) partial compensation for disservices caused by society, such as lifetime disability benefits and medical care to veterans injured in military service; (2) compensation for handicapping conditions, such as special education programs for mentally retarded children and head start programs for children living in poverty; (3) protection for individuals and society, such as health and safety regulations and correctional services for criminals and delinquents; (4) investment in personal or collective advancement, such as universal public education; and (5) immediate or deferred increments to personal well-being, as reflected by individual retirement accounts (IRA) promoted by the federal government, and services provided by art museums, libraries, and parks. Such functions illuminate the complexities involved in determining the bases for social provision in addition to or other than means or income.

Kahn (1969) views the functions of social policy as being expressed in the ideology that underlies the provision of a series of separate social welfare measures under public and voluntary auspices. Such measures, as expressions of social policy, include those of income maintenance, housing, health, education, recreation, manpower and employment, and the personal social services. Like Titmuss, Kahn also perceives that these measures help to shape the quality of life and determine the level of well-being for society's members, as evidenced by increased levels of educational attainment, improved housing conditions and increased economic security for most of society's members, increased longevity, and greater personal freedom.

Other measures that have been identified as also contributing to individual and family well-being are those in the fiscal realm, which Titmuss (1968) labeled *fiscal welfare*. Such measures include tax sheltered savings for individuals and families, earned income tax credits for low-income working parents with preschool children, tax exemptions for dependents, and tax deductions for families who care for elderly and disabled family members at home. Labeling benefits provided through the workplace *occupational welfare*, Titmuss noted that these also contribute to individual and family well-being and potentially have the same effects as measures provided directly by government. Such benefits include health and dental insurance, paid vacations, day care for children of working parents, and parental leave, among others.

Family Policy

FAMILY POLICY AS PERSPECTIVE: CONCEPTS AND DEFINITIONS

If problems of individuals relative to society are the concerns of policy, and the problems of individuals and aggregate relationships are the concerns of social policy, the problems of families relative to society can be said to be the concerns of family policy. As such, family policy may be regarded as a subcategory of social policy. Given Myrdal's (1968) definition that family policy is nothing less than social policy, however, and Kamerman and Kahn's (1978) definition that it is everything government does to and for families, family policy may at once be as broad, or even broader, than social policy in its concerns. Incorporating family well-being as a criterion and standard, family policy introduces family considerations and a family perspective into the policy arena, whether in establishing policy objectives and/or measuring their outcomes.

Policy goals and objectives with respect to families may be *explicit* or *implicit* (Kamerman and Kahn, 1978). Explicit family policies are those in which the goals or objectives for families are deliberately structured. Adoption services, foster care, family planning, programs for battered women, child protection services, maternal and child health, family life education, and day care, are illustrative. Implicit family policies are those that affect families although family objectives are not deliberately structured into them. Examples include special education programs for mentally handicapped children, the retirement test for prospective social insurance beneficiaries, the deinstitutionalization of mentally retarded and mentally ill family members, tax credits for new home buyers, and so forth. Policies in which the objectives or goals for families are explicitly structured also may be regarded as manifest or obvious family policies; implicit family policies, because of their less obvious family dimensions, may be regarded as *latent* family policies. In that most policies in the United States are not explicit as to their family objectives, they are implicit family policies.

Another way to view policies from a family policy perspective is in terms of their family consequences. These may be intended or unintended, direct, or indirect, as well as manifest or latent. The application of these terms not only can help in identifying a sequence of possible effects stemming from a given course of action, but also in anticipating other courses of actions that may need to be taken in light of the effects of the first. For example, while family planning programs have been very effective in attaining their objectives of producing planned and smaller families in the United States, one indirect and unintended consequence of such a policy strategy is a widening of income and opportunity disparities between small and large families. It also has produced a smaller cohort of social security contributors in the years ahead, the effects of which only recently have commanded public attention.

Just as other policy goals and objectives can serve as strategies for achieving policy objectives related to families, family policy can serve as a strategy for achieving goals and objectives not directly related to families, although the latter is not precluded. For example, Gronseth (1967) suggested that the goal of family policy should be to influence the structure and function of the "nuclear extended family," and aim at ensuring a just and reasonable share of income for families with children, thus serving as a stimulant to economic growth. Scanzoni (1983), on the other hand, suggested that family policy should be aimed at achieving greater equity between men and women in their everyday relationships and roles, thereby enabling families to better adapt to a changing world. Such statements reveal how different values can support and reinforce one another when they are congruent, family structures and relationships serving as both policy goals and strategies at one and the same time.

FAMILY POLICY AS A FIELD OF ACTIVITY

Family policy not only represents a perspective, but also a field of activity. As a field, it includes such programs as family planning, food stamp programs, income maintenance programs such as Aid to Families with Dependent Children (AFDC), unemployment compensation, supplemental security income, and so forth; foster care, adoption services, homemaker service, day care, home based parent-aid, and family therapy. In more recent years it also has included employment services, manpower and training programs, housing, health services of various kinds, nutrition programs, child development programs, a range of personal social services, special programs for women, and services for elderly members and their adult children. It also includes a whole body of family law having to do with family relationships and obligations, such as marital rape laws, child support laws, child custody, cohabitation, marriage and divorce, and so forth. The criterion of family well-being, however, extends its domain even further, into such areas of activity as taxation, land use, energy, defense, transportation, the environment, highway safety, and hazardous waste. In other words, as earlier definitions suggest, family policy connotes all activities promoted or sanctioned by government that affect families, directly or indirectly.

Practically and conceptually, therefore, family policy is of relevance to *all* families—not just to particular groups of families, but including them. Thus in applying to all families, it also applies to families in particular circumstances, such as families headed by females, families who are poor, families with young children, families with mentally ill or retarded members, or elderly disabled members (Zimmerman, 1984). Because of the continuing nature of family relationships, it also applies to individual family members, even those with weak family ties.

Concluding Observations

Thus while family policy may be nothing less than social policy, as Myrdal has asserted, its emphasis on families in contrast to individuals is its differentiating characteristic. In this respect, it complements social policy conceptually and adds another dimension to the conceptualization of policy more generally. Indeed, family well-being represents a value that when operationalized can be applied in assessing and evaluating policy in all areas. Its application to policies in areas in which family connections may not be so apparent offers the potential for anticipating negative spillover effects and taking appropriate anticipatory action to minimize them. Warning that countries not having a conscious family policy exposed the family as an important area of social reality to the undesirable impacts of policies in other areas, Myrdal (1968) in fact spoke to the importance of taking such consequences into account.

While the domain of family policy can be broadly or narrowly conceived, family well-being as a value goal may be expected to rank first among other values within its domain, however defined. At the same time, other values, such as equity and freedom, also pertain to issues within family policy, just as they do to issues within policy and social policy more generally. Having outlined the terrain in which this book will be traversing, it is now time to ask: What are the events that have led to thinking about family policy in the United States, especially in light of Schorr's (1972) gloomy account of this country's ambivalent or negative attitude toward policy as it relates to families? To answer this question, the following chapter will focus not only on developments that have contributed to discussion of family policy in this country but also on a way for understanding such developments and this interesting and confusing area of study and action.

References

BAUMHEIER, E. C. and A. L. SCHORR (1977) "Social Policy," pp. 1453-1463 in J. B. Turner, R. Morris, M. N.Ozawa, B. Phillips, B. Schreiber, and B. K. Simon (eds.)

Encyclopedia of Social Work. Washington, DC: National Association of Social Workers.

BOULDING, K. (1967) "The boundaries of social policy." Social Work 12, 1: 3-11.

EASTON D. (1968) "A systems analysis of political life," pp. 428-436 in W. Buckley (ed.) Modern Systems Research for the Behavioral Scientist. Chicago: Aldine.

GIL, D. (1973) Unraveling Social Policy. Cambridge, MA: Schenkman.

GRONSETH, E. (1967) "First national report: Economic family policy and its guiding images in Norway—inconsistencies and consequences," in P. de Bie and C. Presvelous (eds.) National Family Policy Guiding Images and Policies: Transactions of the First International Seminar of the International Seminar of the International Scientific Commission on the Family. Quebec: First International Seminar of the International Scientific Commission on the Family.

KAHN, A. J. (1969) Theory and Practice of Social Planning. New York: Russell Sage Foundation.

KAMERMAN, S. K. and A. J. KAHN (1978) Family Policy: Government and Families in Fourteen Countries. New York: Columbia University Press.

LASSWELL, H. (1968) "The policy orientation," pp. 3-15 in D. Lerner and H. Lasswell (eds.) Policy Sciences. Stanford, CA: Stanford University.

MYRDAL, A. (1968) The Nation and the Family. Cambridge: Massachusetts Institute of Technology.

PEAR, R. (1985) "White House acting to end rules requiring hospitals to help poor." New York Times (Nov. 4): 1Y

REIN, M. (1976) Social Science and Social Policy. New York: Penguin.

SCANZONI, J. (1983) Shaping Tomorrow's Family: Theory and Policy for the 21st Century. Newbury Park, CA: Sage.

SCHORR, A. L. (1972) "Family values and family policy." Journal of Social Policy 1: 33-43.

TITMUSS, R. (1969) Essays on the Welfare State. Boston: Beacon.

———(1968) Commitment to Welfare. New York: Pantheon.

U.S. Bureau of Census (1985) Statistical Abstract of the United States: 1986. 106th edition. Washington, DC. Table 493, pp. 306, 307.

ZIMMERMAN, S. L. (1984) "The mental retardation family subsidy program: Its effects on families with a mentally handicapped child." Family Relations 33,1: 105-118.

CHAPTER 2

Developments in Family Policy: Reflections of Social Change

Anyone who follows the daily newspapers knows that most policy issues are fraught with conflict and contradiction. That this is no less true—and in fact, maybe more true—with respect to family policy should come as no surprise in light of the value traditions that have guided social policy developments in the United States since its beginnings: individualism, minimum government intervention, and private property (Wilensky and Lebeaux, 1965). These traditions have done much to obscure and delay recognition of the connections between families and government in this country. To understand what has led to a growing recognition of their connections is to understand the nature of social change itself. Indeed, when family policy developments are viewed within a framework of social change, some of the confusions and contradictions that are a part of these developments become more understandable (Zimmerman, 1982). For this reason, the framework will be presented before reviewing the phenomena to which it applies in this discussion.

A Framework for Understanding Family Policy Developments in the United States

In the historical development of any society, new ideologies and movements of public opinion emerge within the context of debates about institutionalized cultural values among individuals and groups who act as defenders and advocates of these values (Smelser and Halpern, 1978). Out of such debate, certain value premises emerge as dominant. These become the basis for legitimizing the society's major institutional structures, its normative framework, and system of social control.

The selection of certain value premises over others as the basis for legitimizing society's institutional arrangements creates a situation that is inherently conflictual and contradictory (Smelser and Halpern, 1978). The reasons for this are threefold: (1) different value premises cannot be fully realized simultaneously by those who hold them; (2) values officially sanctioned elicit varying levels of commitment among individuals and groups, particularly in a pluralistic society such as the United States; and (3) the existence of a multiplicity of culturally provided value premises encourages different groups to mobilize and countermobilize around those premises that are more congenial to their situation. Over time, the dominance of competing value themes may be observed to oscillate, with one value theme holding a dominant position in public opinion, social action, and public policy for a period of time, only to be subsequently replaced by another value theme for another period of time. Alternations between conservatism and liberalism in American history are illustrative of these phenomena.

Structural change, which is defined as the introduction of a new or different phenomenon into the society, also contributes to the contradictory and conflictual nature of the situation. To the extent such change diverges from existing normative and cognitive frameworks through which people have come to understand the world in which they live and how they think it should be, it conflicts with them. Thus with the onset of structural change, certain social processes typically begin to unfold. Initially, some individuals and groups begin to express alarm and concern, and begin to define, evaluate, and interpret the new situation to others as they see it. This initial period is likely to be confused because of the multiplicity of culturally provided value premises and perspectives that exist to assign meaning to the new social phenomena. Hence a variety of competing definitions and interpretations of the novel situation is likely to emerge during this initial period. Thus, initially, the struggle is over competing definitions of the situation in which certain individuals and groups play a prominent role.   The cultural struggle precipitated by structural change assumes a political dimension when "moral entrepreneurs" attempt to spread their definition of the situation to politically significant groups, and to mobilize them to press for some kind of purposive social action, or to create such a group in the form of a social movement for this purpose (Smelser and Halpern, 1982). The social action may be a moral crusade, legal regulation, new institution, or organizational reform that accommodates the new definition. This reform or social action may then constitute the condition for initiating another cycle of conflict and change similar to that which gave impetus to it. Through these dynamics, a sequence of oscillating changes may be set off and a series of social forms created as politically significant groups, drawing upon different value premises, respond to threatened interests. The framework diagrammed below serves as a guide for the discussion that follows.

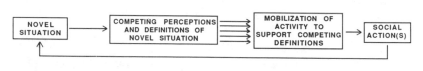

Figure 2.1   Family Policy and Related Developments

VALUE PREMISES UNDERLYING INSTITUTIONAL STRUCTURES AND RELATIONS IN THE UNITED STATES

The values that have guided the development of social policy in the United States are the values that have shaped the ways in which institutional relations between family, government, and the economy have been structured. They also have shaped the ways in which Americans have come to understand the world in which they live and think it should be. These values, as has been noted, are individualism, freedom, and independence. Individualism is both a doctrine that justifies minimal government and a theory of human behavior. As a theory, it assumes that individuals derive pleasure from the acquisition and consumption of material goods and pain from economic loss; that they have biological needs that instinctively cause them to act in their own self-interest; and that the interests of all are served by individuals acting in their own self-interest with little government interference. As a doctrine, it holds that individuals have an obligation to try to get ahead and equal opportunities to do so; that failure in this regard is the fault of the individual, and a source of justifiable shame for both the person and his or her family (Kahn, 1969). Democratic values emphasizing the importance and uniqueness of each individual and embracing the doctrine of "inalienable rights" particularly with respect to life, liberty, and the pursuit of happiness are congruent with individualism. Private property refers to a system of socially recognized and sanctioned rights and duties with respect to the private ownership of valued objects, whether such ownership involves individuals or corporations. It implies the right to buy, use, sell, trade, transfer, destroy, or bequeath a valued object, as the owner deems appropriate (Wilensky and Lebeaux, 1965). Such rights and privileges are associated with free market conditions that promote competition and justify public regulation of economic activity only when its aim is to keep the market free. Under such conditions, individual effort is assessed and rewarded on the basis of efficiency—that is, according to how much it contributes to the production of the most goods and services for the least cost.

Historical conditions of opportunity and mobility that prevailed in this country during the eighteenth and nineteenth centuries supported these value premises (Kahn, 1969). While such conditions tended to reward persons who were industrious and disciplined, they also helped to divert attention from the different circumstances into which people are born. Thus the belief was that those who prospered did so because they were diligent, worked hard, and were virtuous, not because of their family name or circumstances. The family, historically, was not perceived as the means by which people "got ahead and made it" in this country (Kahn, 1969; Wilensky and Lebeaux, 1965; Zimmerman, 1976). Considered a personal, private matter, it was viewed as a separate sphere, occupational advancement taking precedence over family considerations when the two conflicted.

For those who could not take advantage of the opportunities and mobility that prevailing conditions afforded, either because they were too old or were disabled or were too disadvantaged by unfortunate life experiences, the doctrine of individualism had little applicability. Such persons together with the failures, deviants, dropouts, and victims of catastrophe were perceived as "acts of God," to be helped through personal charity and benevolence. Charity as an act of free will and choice not only exemplified the Puritan emphasis on acts of good deeds as evidence of moral worth, but also served as an expression of disdain and distrust for government as an institution. Reinforced by poor law traditions that early settlers brought to this country from Europe, such attitudes emphasized deference in seeking public help by demeaning and stigmatizing those who did. The expectation was that natural networks of immediate and extended family and neighborhood would and should provide help to family members who needed it, despite the fact that such networks often comprised persons who were similarly dispossessed and exploited, leading similarly fragmented and economically marginal lives in similarly demoralized neighborhoods. Thus, bonded by survival needs as much as by love and affection—maybe more — such networks were severely limited in the help they could extend to members (Wilensky and Lebeaux, 1965). Nonetheless, the value premises underlying institutional arrangements with respect to families, government, and the economy—individualism, private property, and minimum government — prevailed as part of the American culture. In practical terms, this meant that people were obliged to work hard and get ahead, that if they needed help, they should get it from their families, or as a last resort, charitable organizations in their own communities, but not government. These were the value premises that formed the ways in which the relationship between families and government was perceived, defined, and structured.

THE NOVEL SITUATION: CHANGES IN INSTITUTIONAL STRUCTURES AND RELATIONSHIPS

Government and the economy

By the 1930s, economic conditions no longer supported the premises underlying the structural relations between families and government. With the Great Depression of the 1930s and the advent of social security, the federal government began to assume an important role in the everyday lives of American families and in the economy. Social security helped not only to stabilize the economic circumstances of families, but by increasing their consumption capacities helped to stabilize the economy as well. By the 1950s and 1960s, the role of the federal government in the social and economic affairs of the country had grown even broader. These years were characterized by relatively steady economic growth with little inflation (Yankelovich, 1982), as evidenced by a 32% increase in the labor force, largely in desirable white-collar jobs, and an unemployment rate among blacks that had declined from 12% in 1961 to 8% in 1970. Such growth, according to Yankolovich, was attributable to more education, more businesses, more research and development, and more educated women entering the work force, all financed out of tax revenues and private investment.

Government spending during these years fueled the economy. Channeling large sums of money into a national highway system through the Highway Trust Fund, government spending stimulated the automobile market. Along with financial assistance to veterans, government expenditures helped to create the suburbs into which many families moved as well as the suburban shopping centers where they shopped. Government loans for education, the GI Bill of Rights, and improved scholarships for students underwrote the expansion in education, education having become the principal means for personal advancement. Government also had broadened its commitments to help those for whom the nation's economic growth mattered little—blacks, elderly, and residual poor. Such commitments included social security, food stamps, education grants and loans, Medicaid and Medicare, AFDC, housing subsidies, and job training programs, all of which directly affected the lives of American families. The civil rights movement, desegregation of schools, and court ordered busing of school children were a part of these years.

By the mid- to late 1970s, after almost three decades of growth and expansion—however erratic—the economy slowed and decelerated (Yankolovich, 1982). Economic opportunities no longer were so plentiful, inflation consumed savings, and the cost of living outstripped disposable income. Key industries such as steel, textiles, and automobiles lost their ability to compete with those of other industrial nations. The oil shortage precipitated by the OPEC nations in 1973 stalled or moved trends downward. At the same time, the annual rate of increase in productivity not only began to decline as the value of the dollar shrunk, but the price of gold skyrocketed. Imports exceeded exports, creating an unfavorable balance of trade. Then in 1979 the threat of a nuclear accident at Three Mile Island eliminated the "nuclear option" as an answer to the energy crisis precipitated by the OPEC countries. But of all these symptoms of a troubled economy, it was inflation that affected American families the most. By 1978, consumer debt rose to 83% of after-tax income. In mid-1980, the stagflation of 1974-1975 reasserted itself. Unemployment increased, especially in manufacturing industries, profits fell with the growth rate, while prices remained high—a situation further complicated by the unpredictability of Third World leaders and nations. It is within this overall context that abortion was legalized, that the women's movement gathered strength, and Vietnam and Watergate became a part of American history.

Families

American families in the meantime had come to expect a continuation of the affluence they had come to enjoy, having grown accustomed to the new freedoms of choice it provided. The counter-culture of the 1960s and the search for self-fulfillment in the 1970s emerged as cultural expressions of the times. As a part of this expression, family came to be viewed as a venture in self-fulfillment and a means of self-realization. While the values and beliefs of the counterculture centered on a simpler life, fewer possessions, a few close relationships, and living close to nature, the values of most American families were consumer-oriented. They wanted more, not fewer material goods and possessions, and more personal freedom, just as the doctrine of individualism in fact decreed.

Such values found expression in changing family structures func-tioning under the constraints of an ailing economy. Women were entering the labor force in increasing numbers. The typical American family consisting of a working father, a mother who stayed at home, and one or two children, which described 70% of all households in the 1950s, by 1980 was representative of only 15% of all households (U.S. Bureau of the Census, 1980). By 1982, almost two-thirds of all married women with children ages 6 to 17 worked outside the home as did almost half of those with children under age 6 (U.S. Bureau of the Census, December 1983a: 414, Table 683). Labor force participation for divorced women was even higher: 84% for mothers with children ages 6 to 17 and 67% for mothers with children under age 6.

Many young adults were postponing marriage. Between 1970 and 1984, the percentage of never married women between ages 25 and 29 more than doubled and almost doubled for men in this age group, representing over one-fourth of all women and well over one-third of all men between ages 25 and 29 (U. S. Bureau of the Census, 1984). The same trend extended to persons in their early thirties, although at about half the rate of those in their late twenties. At the same time, the number of unmarried-couple households quadrupled between 1970 and 1984. In contrast to 1970 when such households were mostly maintained by persons aged 45 years and older, in 1984 they were mostly maintained by persons in their late twenties and early thirties.

The percentage of unmarried young adults living alone or sharing their home with an unrelated adult also increased during this period, as did the percentage of those living at home with their parents. Between 1970 and 1983, the number of young adults living with their parents increased by 85%, with young adults in their late twenties and early thirties again showing the largest increase, 117% (U.S. Bureau of the Census, June 1983: 4). Census Bureau officials indicated that although many of these young adults probably were simply postponing marriage, such trends could indicate that many may not marry at all.   In the meantime, the divorce rate, which continued its long upward trend since the late 1960s, reached an all-time high of 5.3 per 1000 population in 1981 (National Center for Health Statistics, 1985: 1), dropping slightly since then. That contemporary American couples were not staying married "for the sake of the children" was evidenced by the fact that divorcing couples had virtually the same number of children as married couples. Since 1972, the total annual number of children involved in divorce has exceeded 1 million every year, almost doubling in number since 1962, despite the fact that the average number of children per decree dropped from a high of 1.32 in 1965 to a low of .98 in 1980. This meant that fewer children now lived in two-parent families; in 1983 only 75% of all children under age 18 lived with two parents, one of whom may have been a stepparent (U.S. Bureau of the Census, June 1983: 3). In 1983, over one-fifth of all children under age 18 lived in a one-parent family, double the percentage in 1970. The remaining few lived with relatives or friends.

Most one-parent families were and are headed by women. In 1982 one-parent families headed by a woman represented almost one-fifth of all households, more than double what it was in 1960 (U.S. Bureau of the Census, December 1983a: 54, Table 71). For blacks the percentage of female-headed families also more than doubled during this period, but the percentages were much higher: 21% in 1960 and 47% in 1982; in about half of all black households, families are headed by females. Between 1960 and 1982, the proportion of black families headed by never married women tripled, from 11% to 33%, each intervening year showing an increase. The proportion of white families headed by never married women, which fluctuated between 12% and 9% during these years hovered around 11% in 1982, which is what it was for blacks in 1960 (U.S. Bureau of the Census, December 1983a: 54, Table 72).

In addition to all of these changes in family structures, the average life span of family members expanded considerably during these years, attributable in part to improvements in medical technology and nutrition, and greater economic security. At the beginning of the century, less than 10% of the population in the United States lived to be 55 years and older, but by 1982 over one-fifth of the population did (U.S. Bureau of the Census, September 1983: 3, 15, 21). The fastest growing group of the older population was composed of persons 85 years and older, about one-half of whom reported they were limited in their ability to carry on a major activity because of chronic illness, and thus needed assistance from another person to function. Differences in life expectancy for men and women were reflected in their living arrangements: In 1982 five-sixths of all elderly men lived in a family setting, more than three-fourths of whom were married and living with their spouses. In contrast, less than three-fifths of all elderly women lived in a family setting in 1982, of whom only two-fifths were married and living with their spouses, reflecting male/female differences in longevity (men dying earlier than women).

COMPETING DEFINITIONS OF THE NOVEL SITUATION

According to Smelser and Halpern (1978), the initial period of a novel situation is likely to be confused because of the emergence of a variety of competing definitions and interpretations of the situation assigning meaning to the new social phenomena. Thus many viewed the expansion of government's role in the economy and in the lives of families during this period with alarm. They not only regarded it as costly in economic terms, but they also regarded it a threat to individual freedom and family autonomy, a usurpation of family roles and functions. Such a view was expressed by one legislator who, in asserting that government policies had eroded family viability in recent years, opined that the family stands best when it stands alone, not with assorted government crutches (Zimmerman et al., 1979). Indeed, during these years more people had come to regard "big government" as a bigger threat to the country than big business or big labor (Minneapolis Star and Tribune, 1983). Characterizing modern mothers as "quiet, everyday heroes" struggling to stretch family budgets strained by high taxes and inflation, President Reagan called on government "to get off the backs of families" (The New York Times, 1982). To hasten "the return of values and principles that made America both great and good," and restore the family to its "rightful place in society," Reagan advocated lower taxes to stimulate economic growth and opportunities. Some not only advocated lower taxes but also limits on government expenditures, at both state and federal levels, and on taxes that governments could impose as strategies for controlling their spending and growth.

Others viewed the expansion of government not as threat to or usurpation of family roles and functions, but as a development that required an explicit family policy to guide it. The chair of the White House Conferences on Families, for example, in calling for a national family policy asserted that government programs were harmful to families because the United States did not have a national family policy to guide them (Carr, 1979). Indeed, it will be recalled that Myrdal (1968) warned that any country without a conscious family policy "leaves to chance and mischance" an area of social reality of considerable importance, which as a consequence exposes it to the untrammeled and frequently undesirable impact of policies arising in other areas. In keeping with these views, others defined the situation in terms of the functions families perform for their members and society and the support they needed to do so effectively in a changing, unstable environment (Zimmerman, 1980). Alfred Kahn (1969) characterized the family as such a basic and unique institution that the task of protecting and enhancing family life, he said, was in some ways comparable to foreign affairs in the realm of foreign policy and economic affairs in the realm of economic policy.

Others, however, feared that such a policy would result in the loss of personal freedom through the imposition of a national standard on family structures and behaviors (Barbaro, 1978). Others regarded government as too blunt an instrument for dealing with idiosyncratic family issues (Feldman, 1979). Gilbert Steiner (1981), perhaps the most frequently quoted critic of the idea, asserted that family policy would serve no useful purpose, had no viable constituency, and, in essence, was an exercise in futility.

Just as the appropriateness of the expanded role of government was perceived and defined differently by different individuals and groups, so were the changes that had occurred in family structures and life. Many perceived these changes as reflecting a general deterioration in family life and moral values, citing as evidence increasing rates of divorce, increasing numbers of children born outside of marriage, cohabitation without marriage, and labor force participation by mothers with young children. To deal with such perceptions and definitions, advocates called for parental control of school curricula, particularly in the areas of sex and family life education; voluntary prayer in the schools; the return of fault to divorce; and restrictions on second and third marriages, among others (Engelberg et al., 1980). They opposed the Equal Rights Amendment (ERA), abortion, and day care, each of which was perceived as a threat to family values and interests (Kelly, 1980). Such views became evident as early as 1975 when Senator Walter Mondale proposed legislation that would have provided a program of comprehensive services consisting of child care, health, nutrition, recreation, and social services for low-income families (United States Congress, 1975). In 1980, Phyllis Schlafly, leader of the Eagle Forum and organizer of a STOP ERA movement, acting as a "moral entrepreneur" and advocate attempting to persuade others to accept her definition of the situation, charged that working mothers promoted government control of family life by abrogating their family role and demanding publicly sponsored day care. One homemaker, taking issue with the assumption that mothers with young children had to work for wages outside the home, asserted that the needs of children were being sacrificed to the ideology of adult's desires and preferences, which have made being a full-time homemaker an affront to modern society (Zillhardt, 1985).

Feminists, on the other hand, and those sympathetic to gender-role equality and feminist ideology, supported measures opposed by those holding more traditional views, defining the situation differently. For example, the chairperson of a political women's caucus and delegate to the Republican National Convention characterized ERA as a rallying point for supporters who tended to be prochoice and in favor of day care, and domestic violence legislation (Kelly, 1980). In contrast to Phyllis Schlafly, Bella Abzug—noted feminist, former congresswoman, and also a "moral entrepreneur" and advocate for her position— defined ERA not as a family issue but as an economic issue, charging that opposition to ERA came in part from industry, which profited by paying women less than men for the same work.

In short, the expanded role of government and changing family structures were defined and interpreted in a variety of ways, each definition focusing on different dimensions and aspects of the novel situation: too much government, the need for coherence in policies affecting families, burdensome taxes, changing family structures, changing family needs, family disintegration and moral deterioration, women's rights, and children's needs and rights.

MOBILIZATION OF SUPPORT FOR
DIFFERENT DEFINITIONS OF THE NOVEL SITUATION

The activity that mobilized to support different perceptions and definitions of the situation contained its own internal contradictions and conflicts. In his 1976 presidential campaign, President Carter promised to convene a White House Conference on Families as a way of bringing people together from various parts of the country to focus their attention on families and on ways that government might help them (Klauda, 1980). To build support for the conference and thereby assure its realization, an ad hoc coalition was organized consisting of such diverse organizations as the United States Catholic Conference, the National Conference of Catholic Charities, the American Red Cross, the National Association of Social Workers, the Moral Majority, Family America, the National Parent-Teacher Association, the National Council of Churches, the National Urban League, Planned Parenthood, the Synagogue Council of America, and the National Christian Action Coalition. Thus the Ad Hoc Coalition for the White House Conference on Families itself represented a structure of diverse and conflicting interests.

In the meantime, conservative coalitions throughout the country began to organize around the themes of family, decency, and life to rally support for their definition of the situation and normative framework for viewing the relationship between families and government. Using a statement of principles prepared by the National Pro-Family Coalition, pro-life, pro-family, and pro-decency groups sought to dominate state-level meetings to elect delegates to the White House Conference on Families (Meier, 1980). Attendance at the meetings was promoted by religious groups, local churches, special interest groups, and extension agencies that linked their constituencies to larger state and national White House Conference efforts. State-level meetings were polarized concerning the pro-life issue, which for its defenders came to symbolize the family; for protagonists, however, it symbolized an assault on women's rights and freedom of choice.

According to Smelser and Halpern (1978), the cultural struggle precipitated by structural change assumes a political dimension when "moral entrepreneurs" attempt to spread their definitions of the situation to politically significant groups. The extent to which the two major political parties were influenced in the 1980 presidential campaign by the moralists and persuaders of different definitions of changing family structures and expanded government activity may be seen in the family identified planks of their respective platforms (Raum, 1981). The Democrats seemed to favor a definition that emphasized freedom of choice in intimate family matters and supports for the economic functions that families perform; the Republicans supported an opposite one. The two platforms can be compared in Table 2.1.

Regardless of the conflicts over competing perceptions and defi-

TABLE 2.1
1980 Democrat and Republican Platforms

Democrats	Republicans
• Supports ratification of ERA	• Withdraws support for ERA
• Opposes constitutional amendment making abortions illegal and government restrictions on federally funded abortions	• Supports constitutional amendment outlawing abortions and the appointment of judges opposing abortions
• Supports comprehensive national health insurance	• Opposes national health insurance
• Supports a phased-in federal takeover of welfare	• Opposes the federal takeover of welfare
• Supports civil rights for gays	• Supports prayer in the schools
• Opposes benefit reductions in welfare and other human services, including social security	• Supports banning of school busing

SOURCE: Raum (1981). Reprinted with permission of the Minneapolis Star and Tribune.

nitions of the situation, such conflicts signaled an awareness that institutional structures and relations involving families and government had changed over the years. The struggle was over which definition would prevail: the traditional view, which would have tried to change reality to fit the definition, or the view that aimed at changing the definition to fit reality.

SOCIAL ACTION: THE 1980 WHITE HOUSE CONFERENCES ON FAMILIES AND SUBSEQUENT ACTIONS

One of the social actions resulting from the mobilization of activity around competing perceptions and definitions of the novel situation with respect to families, government, the economy, and their relationship to each other was the White House Conferences on Families. Although preparation for the Conferences was filled with controversy and conflict, the conferences took place as scheduled, the conflict shifting to the proceedings. These were filled with charges and countercharges. Attempts by pro-life groups to shape the outcomes of the conferences to meet their definition of the situation met with considerable resistance. In Baltimore, where one of the regional conferences was held, pro-life groups organized walkouts in opposition to delegate recommendations supporting ERA and choice with regard to abortion, charging the conference had been "rigged" to support more government involvement in family life instead of less (Minneapolis Star and Tribune, 1980).

In Minneapolis, a second White House Conference site, the conservative coalition conducted a similar walkout after unsuccessfully attempting to change the voting procedures of the conference to highlight differences between the views of elected and appointed delegates. A dissenter within the conservative caucus charged the caucus with racism, stating that because government often intervened in the lives of black families, wanting government out of family life meant the delegates also wanted black people out of their lives (Byrne et al., 1980). In Los Angeles, the third conference site, similar conflicts occurred, with a National Pro-Family Coalition charging that the conference had been staged to reflect the overrepresentation of social service professionals, federal employees, and bureaucrats, who have a vested interest in government spending (Byrne et al., 1980). An evangelical group met separately to write its own recommendations in an alternative conference (Minneapolis Sunday Tribune, 1980).

Five of the recommendations that failed to win delegate support were those supported by the Pro-Family Coalition (Zack and Klauda, 1980), made up of pro-life groups. The defeated recommendations included anti-ERA and antiabortion measures. Another controversial issue, the definition of family, was resolved through delegate approval of the definition of "two or more persons related by blood, heterosexual marriage and adoption," thus excluding proposals for including homosexual and heterosexual unions not formed through legal marriage, and three-generation families. Many of the 60 recommendations approved by the delegates dealt with economic issues. These included tax credits for homemakers, changes in Medicare and Medicaid regulations to include home care provisions for older and disabled family members, and repealing the marriage tax. Other recommendations called for greater sensitivity to families on the part of government and a systematic analysis of the impact of laws and regulations on families (Klauda, 1980), further acknowledgment of the relationship between families and government.

As a social action that grew out of the mobilization of activity around competing definitions of the situation with respect to families and government and their relationship to each other, the White House

Conferences were important historically, psychologically, and culturally. As the first of such conferences ever held in this country, they not only heightened public awareness of the multitude of ways in which families and government interact, but they also helped to reshape and redefine views about their relationship. By focusing on families, which for so long had been the object of government disregard, they highlighted the importance of the family and made it front page news, and were instigators of some of the actions that followed.   Subsequent to the White House Conferences on Families and flowing directly from them, an Office for Families was created within the Administration of Children, Youth, and Families (Calhoun, 1980). Although allocated a budget of only $120,000, which meant that its role within the federal government was destined to be marginal, the office helped to assure the continued presence of family interests within the federal government. Three years after the White House Conferences on Families, the National Governor's Association (1983) recommended that all policy and legislative proposals be considered from the family's as well as the child's point of view, with first priority given to the enhancement of parental capacities. Consistent with this thrust, a statement issued in 1985 by the Minnesota Governor's Council on Families and Children recommended mandating consideration of families in the formulation and implementation of all legislation and policy by state and contracting agencies.

Other actions subsequent to the White House Conferences on Families reflected a similar definition of the situation relative to the family/government connection. State departments of correction began to train probation officers to work with families of their probationers, a strategy different from previous training and orientation. Similarly, public social service departments began to provide in-home family-based services to prevent the out-of-home placement of abused and neglected children. In the area of health care, hospice programs emphasizing family-centered home care were developed in response to the increased incidence of cancer and other long-term illnesses having a recognizable "terminal period." Increasingly, health and social services began to be delivered to elderly persons in their own home; families increasingly being recognized as ongoing caregivers. Some public agencies modified their organizational structures, combining mental health and child welfare divisions, for example, to better attend to the mental health needs of both families and children. Legislation also was enacted to address many of the recommendations of the White House

Conferences on Families. Examples include the reduction of the marriage tax; financial incentives for families caring for elderly and disabled members at home; the diversion of funding from nursing home and hospital care to community- and home-based services to enable elderly and disabled persons to remain at home; and tax credits for the cost of day care for children of working parents.

COUNTERACTIONS

Family values did not prevail in all actions that followed 1980 White House Conferences on Families, however. Indeed, they did not prevail in most. Such actions include Proposition 13 in California and Proposition 2½ in Massachusetts, tax limitation initiatives that placed a limit on the revenues states could raise through taxes, and thus limits on what state governments could spend to meet family needs. They also include the 1981 Omnibus Budget Reconciliation Act (OBRA), which provided the legal framework for simultaneously cutting federal income taxes and cutting spending for social programs. Such actions reflected perceptions that defined the situation as requiring a diminished role for government in the social and economic affairs of the country along with the restoration of family autonomy and independence—and "strength." Five years later, the Gramm-Rudman- Hollings bill was enacted to eliminate the budget deficits created by the 1981 tax cuts. This bill called for automatic across-the-board cuts in program expenditures if Congress failed to legislate them on its own. Major programs affecting millions of American families were threatened: Medicare, Medicaid, student financial aid, mass transit, antidrug efforts, and community development in addition to those that already have suffered severe cuts. Thus, following Schorr (1972), the family legislation enacted during this period—tax incentives to enable families to care for disabled members at home and tax credits for day-care costs for working parents—may have been actions more consistent with the perception of the need to contain the costs of government than with the perception of the importance of families and the social supports they need to enable them to perform their functions.

NOVEL SITUATION: INCREASING POVERTY, 1980s

As a result of a faltering economy and cutbacks in government spending on social programs, poverty rates, after being relatively stable for over a decade, began to climb again during this period. The 1981-1982 unemployment rate in the United States was higher than at any time since the Great Depression: 9.7%. Families headed by women with no husband present represented a large and growing proportion of the poverty population. In contrast to 1969 when they represented 36% of all families below the poverty level in the United States and only 11% of all families, by 1982 they constituted almost half of all families below the poverty level, and 15% of all families (U.S. Bureau of the Census, December 1983b: 34). For blacks, female-headed families constituted 70% of those who were poor compared with 54% in 1969.

DEFINITION OF THE SITUATION: LATE 1980s

By the late 1980s, another shift in public opinion and definition of the situation appears to be in the making, illustrative of the oscillation in value themes and perceptions of problems that occurs over time. Former liberals who supported cutbacks in government spending and a smaller role for the federal government in 1980 now appear to be worried about new manifestations of old problems: the growing underclass of women and children, increasing disparities in income, and increasing rates of poverty (Bremmer, 1984; Johnson, 1984; Institute for Research on Poverty, 1984; The New York Times, 1982). In addition, they were beginning to have difficulty reconciling the contradictions in the conservative definition of the situation requiring a strong government in foreign affairs supported by a strong military, but a weak government with little social responsibility in domestic affairs (Broder, 1985). They similarly were beginning to find conservative appeals for a constitutional amendment to prohibit abortion and legislation to permit voluntary prayer in the schools along with Baby Doe reporting requirements difficult to reconcile with conservative appeals for getting government out of family life. Senator Daniel Moynihan (1985) defined the situation of increasing poverty among children in female-headed families as one that requires a national family policy, and could emerge as one of the "moral entrepreneurs" of this period in trying to persuade others to accept this definition of the situation.

Conclusion

Thus social action with regard to the family/government connection appears to be a continuing process with one set of values premises prevailing at one time or in some instances, and at other times, another set of values prevailing. Helping to unravel some of the confusions and contradictions of family policy developments, the application of a framework of social change helps to make the process more understandable. By illuminating the confusions and contradictions of family policy developments, the framework also highlights the complexities of these developments and their interactive nature as part of the process of social change itself. The extension of observations to include related events or actions beyond the White House Conferences on Families or simultaneous with them, highlights the number of competing definitions that can be supported at any one time in different streams of actions. As will be recalled, this is possible because of the number of socially sanctioned values our pluralistic culture provides and the multiplicity of action centers that are structured into government as an institution. Thus family policy developments in the United States can be expected to be observable on many different levels in many different forms, not all of which may be congruent or consistent with the others. All of them, however, can be expected to reflect activity that has been mobilized around particular definitions of the relationship between families and government. In this regard the framework of social change should be modified to reflect the number of levels and points within the same level at which change can occur, and the fact that change involves simultaneous actions and counteractions.

Because the social change framework is constructed around institutional structures and relations and the value premises that underlie them, it is very much tied to the institutional perspective for understanding family policy. How are these value premises reflected in government structures? Of what consequence has this been for family policy in the United States? These are the questions that the following chapter will address.

References

BARBARO, F. (1978) "The case against family policy." Social Work 24, 6: 455-459.
BREMMER, H. (1984, June 27) Statement before the Joint Economic Committee of U.S. Congress.
BRODER, D. S. (1985) "Conservative thinkers react against Reaganism." Minneapolis Star and Tribune (November 3): 26A.
BYRNE, C., B. BENIDT, and C. HUDGINS (1980) "Family feud." Minneapolis Star (June 20): 1A.
CALHOUN, J. A. (1980) "The office of families: a beginning." COFO Memo (Spring/Summer III) 2: 5.

CARR, J. (1979) "WHCF: an update." COFO Memo (Winter II) 2.
ENGELBERG, S., P. LANGLEY, and K. SANSOM (1980) "Family Protection Act S1808." COFO Memo (Spring/Summer II): 7.
FELDMAN, H. (1979) "Why we need a family policy." Journal of Marriage and Family 41, 3: 453-456.
IRP Focus (1984) "Poverty in the United States: where do we stand now?" 7, 1: 1-13. Institute for Research on Poverty, Madison, WI.
JOHNSON, H. (1984) "The growing gap between the haves and have nots." Minneapolis Star and Tribune (March 2): 15A.
KAHN, A. J. (1979) Social Policy and Social Services. New York: Random House.
———(1969) Theory and Practice of Social Policy. New York: Russell Sage Foundation.
KELLY, M. C. (1980) "ERA battle plans." Minneapolis Star and Tribune (June 4): 17A.
KLAUDA, P. (1980) "Conference on Families filled Carter campaign pledge." Minneapolis Star and Tribune (June 27): 6f, 8f.
MEIER, P. (1980) "Anti-abortion forces dominate state meetings on families." Minneapolis Star and Tribune (January 25): 1A.
Minneaplois Star and Tribune (1983) "Government rated as top threat of 3 bigs." July 14: 8A.
———(1980) "Conservatives walk out of White House Family Conference." June 27: 8D.
Minneapolis Sunday Tribune (1980) "Family delegates rank issues." (July 13): 12A.
MOYNIHAN, D. P. (1985, April 8-9) "Family and nation: The Godkin lectures." Cambridge, MA: Harvard University. (mimeo)
MYRDAL, A. (1968) Nation and Family. Cambridge, MA: MIT Press.
National Center for Health Statistics (1985, February 28) 1982 Monthly Vital Statistics Report. Vol. 33, No. 11, Supp. DHHS Pub.(PHS) 85-1120 (Advance report of final divorce statistics). Hyattsville, MD: Public Health Service.
National Governor's Association (1983, August) Committee on Human Resources.
RAUM, T. (1981) "Definite difference evident in GOP, Democratic platform." Minneapolis Star and Tribune (August 14): 1C.
SCHORR, A. L. (1972) "Family values and public policy." Journal of Social Policy 1, 1: 33-43.
SMELSER, N. and N. J. HALPERN (1978) "The historical triangulation of family, economy and education," pp. S288-S316 in J. Demos and S. S. Boocock (eds.) Turning Points: Historical and Sociological Essays in the Family. Chicago: University of Chicago Press.
STEINER, G. (1981) The Futility of Family Policy. Washington, DC: Brookings Institution.
The New York Times (1983) "Reagan links his policy to help for the family." (May 8): 10Y.
———(1982) "Study: U.S. policies like those of 1930s." (September 14): 9A.
U.S. Bureau of the Census (1984) Current Population Reports Series P-20, No. 391. Households, Families, Marital Status and Living Arrangements: March (Advance report).
———(1983a, December) Statistical Abstract of U. S.: 1984 (104th edition). Washington, DC: Government Printing Office.
———(1983b, December) Current Population Reports P-23, No. 130. Population Profile of United States, 1982. Washington, DC: Government Printing Office.
———(1983, September) Current Population Reports P-23, No. 128, America in Transition: An Aging Society. Washington, DC: Government Printing Office.
———(1983, June) Current Population Reports Series P-20, No. 389, Marital Status and Living Arrangements, March 1983. Washington, DC.
———(1980) American Families and Living Arrangements (prepared for White House Conference on Families). Chart 19, p. 12.
United States Congress (1975) S626 Child and Family Services Act of 1975.
WILENSKY, H. and C. N. LEBEAUX (1965) Industrial Society and Social Welfare. New York: Free Press.

YANKELOVICH, D. (1982) New Rules: Searching for Self-Fulfillment in a World Turned Upside-Down. New York: Bantam.

ZACK, M. and P. KLAUDA (1980) "Unity plea opens family meeting." Minneapolis Tribune (June 20): 1A.

ZILLHARDT, J. (1985) "When the needs of children take second place to the wishes of adults." Minneapolis Star and Tribune (November 23): 19A.

ZIMMERMAN, S. L. (1982) "Confusions and contradictions in family policy developments: application of a model." Family Relations 31, 3: 445-455.

———(1980) "The family: building block or anachronism." Social Casework 61, 4: 195-204.

———, P. Mattessich, and B. Leik (1979) "Legislators' attitudes toward family policy." Journal of Marriage and Family 41, 3: 507-517.

CHAPTER *3*

An Institutional Perspective
for Understanding Family Policy

To talk about family policy developments in relation to changing institutional structures is to talk not only about social change, but also about policy as the outcome of the ways in which government as an institution is structured. According to institutionalists, an institutional perspective can help to explain much of what happens or does not happen with regard to policies affecting families. As Dye notes (1975), policy does not exist until it is enacted, implemented, and enforced by some governmental agency.

Definitions, Concepts, and Assumptions

What is the institutional perspective with respect to policy and what is its relevance to family policy in particular? Policy from the institutional perspective is defined as the outcome of institutional arrangements governed by norms that tend to persist over time (Dye, 1975). Norms are rules that help to control and predict human behavior and set standards for institutional activity. Norms with respect to the federal government are embedded in the Constitution, which specifies its role, relationships, and the nature of its activities. This includes its role relative to the states and the people; the role of its chief executive, the president, and his or her relationship to Congress; the role of its legislative body, Congress, and the relationship of the Senate and House of Representatives to each other; the role of the judiciary; and the role of citizens. It also outlines the rights and obligations of each of the three branches of government with respect to the formulation, implementation, and enforcement of policy, as well as the relationship among federal, state, and local governments.

The basic assumptions underlying institutional arrangements in the United States with respect to government, as outlined in the Declaration of Independence, are that (l) all persons are created equal and have certain inalienable rights, among which are life, liberty, and the pursuit of happiness; (2) that to ensure these rights, individuals create governments that derive their power from the consent of the governed; (3) that governments are responsible for carrying out the collective preferences of citizens whose fortunes and lives are seen as being bound to each other; (4) that whenever any government becomes destructive of these ends, the people have the right to change or abolish it, and to institute a new government based on principles that seems to have the greatest likelihood of ensuring the safety and happiness of all citizens; (5) and that to prevent the usurpation of individuals' rights, a system of checks and balances in the form of the separation of executive, legislative, and judicial powers is necessary. These are the norms, values, and assumptions that have guided the relationship between families, government, and social policy in the United States as it relates to families, to which reference was made in the previous chapter.

Government policy as the outcome of patterned institutional activity is distinguished by its legitimacy, universality, and authority. Legitimacy pertains to the legal obligation of citizens to comply with the law; universality to the applicability of such obligation to all persons within the society; and authority to the nature of sanctions that can be imposed to enforce the law, namely, fines and imprisonment. While such distinctions are useful, some qualifiers are necessary. For example, the term *universal* is more characteristic of some government policies than others, such as those related to social security, civil rights, education, and taxation. It is less characteristic of policies related to public welfare, such as AFDC, which by their nature are particularistic in terms of the objects they are intended to affect. Further, institutions such as the family and religion also have the means to impose sanctions on members who violate institutional rules or norms. In the case of the family, such sanctions may take the form of the withdrawal of love or an inheritance, and in the case of some religious institutions, ex-communication—both of which can have devastating effects on members. Thus the nature of the sanctions that institutions can impose are different, government being the only institution that can restrict the individual's right to freedom via involuntary imprisonment for failure to comply with the law.

Implications for Family
Policy at the Federal Level

What are the implications of the institutional perspective for family policy? Of what consequence are the norms ruling the way government is structured as well as structure itself for family policy? On the assumption that an explicit family policy was needed to promote conditions supportive of families, Alfred Kahn and his colleagues (Kahn et al., 1979) undertook an analysis of government structure at the federal level. Implicit in their assumption was that such policy would protect basic family functions such as childbearing, child rearing, and family caregiving, without imposing norms of conformity that would negate essential values with respect to family privacy, individual rights, and freedom, or the pluralism and diversity that are a part of the American culture and present institutional arrangements.

What Kahn and his colleagues discovered was that although many of the 385 committees and subcommittees in the House and Senate had some responsibility for some family issue or concern, none had a general overall interest in families or family well-being more broadly. Nor did any of the various agencies of the federal government. Because committees were created in response to concerns expressed by different groups, they were generally found to represent narrow special interests. Having been created out of special interests, they tended to maintain and foster competition between and among competing groups representing the competing needs of family members, the demands and needs of elderly members competing with the needs of children, and the special needs of families with retarded members with the special needs of families with mentally ill members—all of whom were in competition for legislative support and dollars. Constituent demands that congressional representatives be advocates and ombudspersons rather than statespersons only intensified such competition and fragmentation. Thus the lack of coherence in family policy, or any other area for that matter, is an understandable outcome of the norms underlying government's structure.

Another impediment to the institutionalization of broader family interests within the federal government cited by Kahn et al. was the organization of state and federal governments around functions— health, income maintenance, housing, social services, education, and employment and manpower—and, in the case of the federal government, defense—rather than around population groups, as Senator

Moynihan (Congressional Record, 1986) has advocated. Yet, previous experience in this country in trying to organize programs and services around populations, such as the elderly or children, was not particularly noteworthy (Kahn et al., 1979), except in relation to legislative oversight, the collection and dissemination of information, and the mobilization of legislative support. The experience of other countries in trying to incorporate broader family interests within government structures was not encouraging, either. According to one foreign observer of such efforts, if family interests are broadly defined, they are too all encompassing for a single government agency, but if they are too narrowly defined, the sphere of government activity is so restricted that little could be achieved (Kahn et al., 1979). Seen in this light, the creation of an Office on Families to represent broader family interests within the federal government can be regarded as an attempt to institutionalize other norms to govern the structure. The creation of the House Select Committee on Families and Children and the proposal to create a similar committee in the Senate do as well. Such a committee in the Senate, Senator Moynihan has argued, would help expose certain trends that traditional arrangements tend to conceal, thereby enabling the Senate to discern family trends earlier (Congressional Record, 1986).

Implications for Family
Policy at the State Level

Just as efforts have taken place at the federal level to structure broader family interests into the pattern of ongoing government activities, efforts have also taken place at the state level, according to findings of a mail survey of the 50 states (Zimmerman, 1987). The survey was conducted to determine how many states had family councils within their structures, the family policy issues of greatest concern to them, and the family legislation states enacted in the mid-1980s. The assumption was that structure *would* make a difference, that is, that the outcomes would be different in states that did and did not have such councils in terms of the family issues they supported and the family legislation they enacted. Of the 46 states that responded, 14 indicated they had no such entity within their governments' structure. Of the 32 that did, 6 were governor's councils, 6 interagency coordinating councils, 7 legislators' legislative committees, and 25 "other" committees organized around a potpourri of specific family issues. Most of the committees were lodged within governors' offices, others in Departments of Human Services. Regardless of where they were located, for the most part, governors appointed members. Functions most commonly performed by the councils were the oversight of legislation pertinent to families, followed by the conduct of studies related to issues relevant to families, and advocacy and lobbying on behalf of family-related legislation.

According to the frequency with which individual issues were mentioned, the top priority issue for all states and committees in 1985—regardless of whether they had a council or not, or the type of council they had—was child abuse. Adolescent pregnancy, drinking and driving, and foster care were the next most important issues for all states and committees except the interagency coordinating committees. Curiously, the committee type showing the broadest range of family concerns was the one labeled "other," the only committee type identifying educational reform and economic development as priority issues for states in open-ended responses. However, despite the failure of most respondents to mention it in their open-ended responses, their scaled ratings of 43 individual issues indicated that economic development was an issue of top priority to states in 1985. The rated importance of economic development was followed by child protection, educational financing, and cost containment in health care in order of descending importance. Issues rated least important to states in order of descending importance were: public transportation, high interest rates, and suicide, followed by divorce laws, prayer in the schools, health standards for farm workers, and finally, euthanasia. T-test analysis showed that variations in the ratings of issues could not be attributed to structure, that is, according to whether states did or did not have family councils.

The later classification of the 43 individual issues into 7 categories in order to be able to assess the relative importance of explicit family issues to states showed that family issues and economic issues as grouped issues tied for second place in ranked importance to states. Grouped issues ranking highest in importance pertained to program financing; those tying for third place included environmental and educational issues, and issues pertaining to social problems such as homelessness and driving while drinking. Farm issues ranked fourth in importance to states. T-tests again showed that variations in responses could not be attributed to structure, that is according to states that did and did not have a council.

The legislation that states enacted in 1985 encompassed topics far wider ranging than the legislative agendas of any of the committees. When asked to specify the legislation their states enacted in 1985 that directly affected families, most respondents identified legislation that was explicit in its family concerns: adoption, foster care, child protection, child abuse, domestic violence, child support, child care, child health, and juvenile delinquency. Child abuse, which was a priority issue of both states and committees, legislatively outstripped all other family-related issues in 1985 in terms of the frequency with which it was mentioned (N = 64) followed by child support legislation, judicial proceedings for juveniles, child care, adoption, family/elderly abuse, missing children, and health care benefits. In assessing whether states that had councils differed from states that had no councils in terms of the family legislation states enacted, it was curious to note that the latter reported the enactment of more child care and health care legislation than did states having councils. Except for these two instances, however, whether or not states had a council seemed to make no difference in terms of their legislative achievements relative to family issues.

Despite the inability to discern differences in policy outcomes based on the ways in which state governments were structured to attend to family issues, the councils were perceived as being very important in influencing states' legislative program vis-à-vis families by most respondents in states that had them. Some respondents, in elaborating on their responses, took an institutional approach, referring to both the legislative mandate for their committee and committee composition in explaining why they thought it was so important. One respondent reported that when the committee worked throughout the year to create an awareness of issues, and worked with others to write, endorse, and pass legislation, "the result was phenomenal," indicating that the structure facilitated both process and outcomes. Just as respondents who rated the councils lower in importance cited the functions the councils performed—advocacy, monitoring, and advisory—those who rated the councils higher in importance did also. Those who gave the councils higher ratings mentioned their role in identifying problems and mobilizing support within the legislative and executive branches of state government for needed services; in drafting and reviewing legislation in conjunction with the governor's office; and in helping to increase the amount of legislation related to families, children, and youth enacted by states.

That differences could not be discerned between states having and not having such structural arrangements in terms of policy outcomes vis-à-vis family issues could be interpreted in several ways: (1) such structures actually were less important than the institutional perspective assumes and that respondents in states having such structures perceived or were willing to acknowledge; (2) states not having family councils had other structural arrangements for carrying out functions the councils performed that the study did not identify; (3) differences among states in the legislation they enacted were diminished by the nature of federal-state relations; and, finally, (4) given the nature of the study, such differences could not be discerned.

Case Studies of State-Level Experiences in Incorporating Broader Family Concerns

Because of their ties to the governors' office, legislature, and administrative departments, family councils have access to the highest levels of state government. For this reason, their activities are constrained by the political bureaucracy into which they are structured, which makes them vulnerable to changes in institutional leadership or administration (Children's Defense Fund, 1983). The case of the Massachusetts Office of Children is illustrative. The Office was created by statute during a period of service expansion to gather and disseminate information to influence the enactment of legislation on behalf of children and their families. The premise was that information was a powerful resource for this purpose (Aber, 1983). Although the Office of Children had become effective in doing what it was created to do, the skills it had developed were no longer needed or wanted during the period of retrenchment that followed. Thus despite its close ties to important policymakers within state government, and its position within the executive office of the Department of Human Services, the Secretary of Human Services introduced legislation on behalf of the administration in both the 1980 and 1981 sessions to dismantle the Office. Although the local councils whose activities the state Office coordinated rose to the occasion by lobbying on behalf of the state Office and gained a one-year reprieve, by 1985 the Office of Children no longer appeared on the organization chart of Massachusetts' state government.

Minnesota's experience was different in that one of the over 100 different commissions the governor created within a two-year period in the early 1980s was a Council on Families and Children. Involving scores of people in the political process, such commissions helped to create a cadre of supporters for the governor and his program that crossed party lines, enabling him to deal with and defuse highly controversial issues (Wilson, 1985). Further, by creating a sense of purposeful activity, they gave the impression that action was being taken on problems. The governor, in defending his heavy use and reliance on such committees, argued that they enabled competing groups to come together to focus their attention on the "betterment of the state."

The Governor's Council on Families and Children was made up of 15 members appointed by the governor, all except one or two being professionals. They represented such diverse interests as child health, day care, mental health, mental retardation, juvenile justice, and such entities as corporations, small business, the university, and Hispanic and black populations. The governor charged the council to prepare a legislative agenda for families for the his review and perhaps espousal. To be advisory to the governor on family matters, the council was to function as a conduit for the flow of information into and out of government relative to family matters by holding hearings and conducting surveys, and also by being a focal point for citizen input. In addition, the council was instructed to prepare a family impact statement for guiding government activities as they intersected with families. That the governor took no note of the work of the council under the administration that immediately preceded his speaks to the lack of continuity that is structured into the institutional practices and processes of government.

In contrast to previous councils that were lodged in the Governor's Office, the present council was lodged within the Department of Human Services. The advisory nature of its role relative to the governor and commissioner of the Department of Human Services precluded its use of public advocacy to promote its positions. Further, although its organizational relationship to the governor and commissioner of the Department of Human Services was direct, as was its relationship to related departments of health, employment security, education, and so forth, such relationships were mediated by council staff. While members were encouraged to meet with legislators and meetings were arranged where this might occur, these were managed by council staff, relegating members to a somewhat passive role.

Although the legislative agenda adopted by the council could be viewed as representative of the council's position in that it reflected group consensus, the council's position also reflected the interests of the Department of Human Services and of individual legislators whose views the council came to support. The following list details the council's 1985 agenda:

1. Establishment of a Children's Trust Fund to support community-based efforts to prevent child abuse and neglect with monies for the fund coming from a voluntary income tax check-off.
2. Creation of a sliding fee scale for child care to subsidize child-care expenses of low-income parents for whom the costs of child care were a barrier to employment.
3. Passage of "Birth through Three" legislation to expand the definition of school age for handicapped children from birth to age 21 in order to make educational services available to them both earlier and longer.
4. Early childhood and family education legislation expanding the definition of "parent" to include "expectant parent," thereby expanding eligibility for participation in family education programs.
5. Creation of a Catastrophic Health Expense Protection Program, appropriating monies to fund the Catastrophic Health Insurance Program so that families may receive help in meeting the costs of a single episode of unusually high medical expense.
6. Awarding of Permanency Planning Grants to counties providing family-based services.
7. Establishment of Transitional Care for Children with Catastrophic Illness, creating a care unit outside the hospital setting for children whose medical condition had stabilized, offering live-in facilities for parents, ongoing therapy for the children, and instruction to parents concerning the management of at-home care.

Of these bills, the three that passed unequivocally were the sliding fee scale for child care for low-income parents, early childhood and family education, and the permanency planning grants. The Children's Trust Fund, which was placed on the legislative agenda again in 1986, was defeated because its funding was dependent on a voluntary income tax check-off, a funding mechanism that many legislators considered inappropriate in light of the seriousness of the problem it addressed—child abuse. The Birth through Three legislation, while it did not pass as originally proposed, did succeed in lowering the definition of "school age" to age three for mentally retarded children. A bill to extend the definition to birth was proposed again in the 1986 session. Although the bill to provide transitional care for children with catastrophic illness did not pass as proposed, access to state maternal and child health funds was made available to all counties, some of which can be used to provide transitional care. The only bill the council supported that the legislature did not was the Catastrophic Health Expense Protection Program bill, although it too was on the legislature's agenda again in 1986. None of these bills were written or developed by the council.

Because so much of the council's agenda was shaped by council staff, one question that arose with respect to the structural arrangements the council represented was whether staff could not have performed some of the same functions without the council as with it. That is, was such a structure needed to monitor and disseminate information about legislation of importance to families and to get input from citizens about it? The perception was that the council structure was necessary for these activities, that it served to legitimize staff activities, and gave sanction to staff appearances before the legislature in testifying on behalf of families and the council's legislative program. Because the council was perceived to be neutral in allegiance, it also was perceived as helping to foster cooperative interagency relationships among departments of health, education, employment security, and human services.

Whether the council could have been more effective had it been an independent, autonomous entity was another question that arose. As a state advisory group funded by the state legislature, the council was not required to seek out and search for resources to support its activities, and thus could concentrate its attention on substantive issues. Further, having a staff member who was an "insider," privy to insider's knowledge, meant that legislative negotiations and bargains struck could be easily monitored with respect to their implications for the council's legislative agenda. Also, threats to favored items could be more confidently protected from adverse legislative action because of the ongoing presence of council staff. Its financial and political dependency, however, as outcomes of its institutional ties to the legislature, operated to constrain its choice of legislative issues to support and promote and the ways in which it did so.

This was revealed by the way in which the four hearings the council held in different parts of the state were managed. For example, to inform people about the "hearings," the council placed announcements in local newspapers in the communities in which the hearings were held, as it was legally required to do. In addition, however, it mailed special announcements to selected individuals and organizations: those who had attended previous Governor's Conferences on Families, agency staff, and representatives from selected statewide organizations, inviting them to make statements relative to five areas of legislative concern for the council: child care, AFDC, health, education, and children and the law. Most of those who attended the hearings were service providers, some of whom also were parents. In general, those who were "just" parents, representing purely parental interests, did not attend any of the four council hearings.

The hearings were controlled not only through the mailing lists and their agendas, but also by the way they were structured. A larger group of 35 who attended one meeting was divided into smaller groups of four, ostensibly to encourage discussion and elicit recommendations with respect to the five areas of council concern outlined above. While such a strategy indeed may have served to promote discussion, it also served to diffuse potential conflict and antagonisms.

The outcome of the process was a report of the hearings that was forwarded to the governor. It represented a potpourri of views and opinions about government's role with respect to different aspects of family life: teenage pregnancy, divorce, AFDC, tax deductions for dependent children, tax incentives to enable mothers to remain at home with preschool children, the politicalization of family issues, regulations that unduly restricted access to benefits, disincentives for working while on AFDC, making education a priority over public welfare in appropriations, health care prevention measures, the high cost of health care, the high cost of poor health, individual responsibility for one's health, high infant mortality rates, health care delivery, the importance of the school nurse and paraprofessionals in health care delivery, health care consumer education, health maintenance organizations, cost containment, statewide consistency in health care provision, and so on. It considered a range of child-care issues that included concerns of quality, cost, standards, government monopoly of child care, family life education, parent abdication of parental role, discipline, overburdened schoolteachers, parent involvement, child abuse and neglect, teenage suicide, teenage mothers, legal procedures that prevented timely interventions, excessive use of out-of-home placements, the rights of families, and dissemination of information about resources for troubled families.

The advisory nature of the council and its lack of authority were reflected in the family impact statement it prepared and submitted to the governor for his consideration. An initial draft, taken in part from a family impact statement prepared by the government in Quebec, "required" the state to show consideration of families in the development and implementation of legislation, policies, and services. Discussion centered on the word *required*; some members expressed the view that, given the council's advisory status and lack of authority, the term was somewhat presumptuous. Other members felt that it was because of the council's advisory status and lack of authority that the term should be used, rejecting the suggestion to substitute the word "encourage" for "require." Whether or not the statement was adopted by the governor and the legislature seemed to be less of an issue for council members than the opportunity to exercise whatever authority their role as council members allowed.

A County-Level Experience in Incorporating Family Interests

The more broadly defined role of the state Council on Families and Children discussed above contrasts markedly with the more narrowly defined role of a county-level task force that a board of county commissioners convened to review mental health services for families and children and to make recommendations regarding such services (Hennepin County Community Services Department, 1986). The group comprised representatives from different departments of county government, private agencies, interest and advocacy groups, mental health professionals, and academic specialists. The task force chair was the director of the department responsible for the delivery of mental health services for families and children in the county. In his instructions to the task force, he cautioned that its recommendations be confined to those that could be implemented by the county agency, or the agencies with which it contracts for services.

The director as chair guided the process. It began with a series of informational meetings regarding the mental health problems of families and children that have come to the attention of the agencies providing services under contract with the county agency. These were followed by a series of meetings involving the nominal group process to develop a list of problems, categories of problems, and a rank order of problems within the categories. Out of this process, the group developed a series of recommendations for action, based on the problems identified in the meetings and group discussion. The mental health service system for families and children was conceptualized in the task force report as a network of interrelated individuals, organizations, rules, and activities that included the following:

(1) families and children with or directly affected by mental health problems;
(2) agencies and groups serving families and children, including individual mental health professionals; and
(3) statutes, rules, policies, and practices with respect to the provision and funding of intervention and treatment services.

Illustrative of how institutional arrangements shape institutional outcomes, the task force report noted that family and children's mental health services, lacking visibility and distinctiveness, reflected the diffusion of service accountability and case responsibility over several service providers. The task force noted that present institutional arrangements presented significant service coordination and case management problems within the service continuum. It was not at all unusual, the report said, for several providers to have a high degree of involvement with a client at any single time, as well as over time. The absence of a centralized case management role within the agency was identified as a problem for the provision of timely and appropriate service linkages and transitions through the service continuum. Also identified as problems were funding and financing arrangements that encouraged focusing attention on the most difficult situations while diverting attention from those that required less intensive services or situations in which preventive services might help. Such funding patterns also led to the premature termination of services and treatment and/or difficulty in obtaining needed services. The development of the task force's recommendations involved a considerable amount of staff time and discussion. Although the process was guided by staff, as was true for the advisory Council on Families and Children at the state level, the connection between the group's recommendations and agency's future actions was more evident in the case of the county agency. This in part may have been attributable to the direct involvement of the director in the process and the centrality of the issue to his and the county's concerns, as well as to the specificity of the task force's mission. Pertinent to this discussion was the task force's definition of family mental health as both a perspective and a set of discrete services, reminiscent of the definition of family policy.

Discussion and Conclusion

The institutional perspective helps to illuminate the ways in which structure affects policy as process and outcome at all levels: federal, state, and county. Efforts to create structures within government that reflect broader, rather than narrower, family interests reflect concerns that institutional norms and structures are obstacles to the development of more coherent and responsive family policies. Given this perspective, however, the pallid nature of outcomes that emerged from the patterned activities of the institutional structures represented by the state family councils and county task forces are hardly surprising. That such structures may serve functions other than the promotion of family legislation may help to explain findings from a 50-state survey showing that for the most part, states that had family councils did not enact more family legislation than states that did not, nor did they differ in terms of the issues they considered of high priority. That councils are constrained in terms of the issues they support and the ways in which they do so can be understood in terms of their institutional ties to the political bureaucracy. From an institutional perspective, such ties also help to explain the very different experiences of the Minnesota and Massachusetts councils, although they do not explain differences in the attitudes of the governors of these states toward the councils. Also, the institutional perspective does not provide a way of knowing whether the controlled management of institutional activities is more attributable to the style and personality characteristics of the persons involved or the norms that govern such activities.

Thus the institutional perspective and the concepts it employs— values, norms, roles, patterns of behaviors and activities, continuity over time, structures, and structural arrangements—while helping to account for some outcomes of government activity relevant to family policy, is unable to account for all outcomes of such activity. It also does not provide the concepts for understanding the substance of family policy. Thus other frameworks are needed to understand more fully family policy as substance and process. Such frameworks are the focus of the chapters that follow.

References

ABER, J. L. (1983) "The role of state government in child and family policy," in E. F. Zigler et al. (eds.) Children, Families, and Government. New York: Cambridge University Press.

Children's Defense Fund (1983, July) CDF Reports: Children's forums growing within state government. Washington, DC: Author.

Congressional Record (1986, February 3) "Establishing a special committee on family, youth and children." Proceedings and Debates of the 99th Congress, p. 330.

DYE, T. (1975) Understanding Public Policy. Englewood Cliffs, NJ: Prentice-Hall.

Hennepin County Community Services Department (1986, January) Final Report and Recommendations of the Hennepin County Family and Children's Mental Health Task Force. Minneapolis, MN: Author.

KAHN, A., S. KAMERMAN, and M. DOWLING (1979) Government Structure Versus Family Policy. New York: Columbia University Press.

WILSON, J. (1985) "Citizen panel payed practical dividends for Perpich." Minnesota Star and Tribune (February 6): 1B.

ZIMMERMAN, S. L. (1987) States' Councils on Families and/or Children: Form or Substance: A Report of a Survey of the 50 States. St. Paul: University of Minnesota.

PART II

FRAMEWORKS FOR UNDERSTANDING POLICY/FAMILY CONNECTIONS

CHAPTER 4

Policy Frameworks for Understanding Family Policy

While the social change model permits observations of changes in the structural arrangements that govern institutional relationships between families, government, and the economy, and the institutional perspective permits family policy to be seen in relation to these arrangements—which to some extent helps to explain why the United States has no coherent family policy—other policy frameworks permit insights into other dimensions of family policy. These are frameworks that view policy as rational choice, as incremental choice, as choice under competitive situations, as the equilibrium reached among contending interest groups, and as elite preferences. Each already has been introduced in various ways, both in the definitions of policy and in the recounting of the White House Conferences on Families, and even in the discussion that approaches family policy from an institutional perspective. This indicates that policy as substance and process probably represents the full range of perspectives on any given issue, and that the treatment of each separately should be regarded for analytical purposes only.

Policy as Rational Choice

Of all the frameworks, the one that views policy as rational choice probably represents the ideal. The classical model of rational choice perceives rational action as consisting of choice and action relative to the optimal means for achieving a given goal (Frohock, 1979) and that the alternative selected will be the one that maximizes the values most relevant to the situation (Dye, 1975). The model assumes that all relevant values are known and that choosing a course of action requires the sacrifice of some values in order to achieve others. Implicit in the model are knowledge and understanding of the factors that circumscribe the range of alternatives that can be considered in selecting a course of action to address a problem. Such factors include the socioeconomic, cultural, and historical context of the choice situation, including the attitudes, psychological predispositions, and shared values of a population and its stage of economic development. Also implicit in the model is consistency in the application of values or principles for selecting the best or optimal alternative and strategies for implementing it. Because the model seeks to maximize all social, political, and economic values, not just those that lend themselves to numerical counting, it also implies efficiency.

The basic concepts of all rational action models include: goals and objectives; their consequences; alternative goals and objectives and their consequences; and finally, choice, decision, or action. The values underlying the selection of goals and strategies for achieving them, as has been stated, refer to whatever the larger society and the social aggregates comprising it deem most important. Such values include: equality, equity, rights, freedom, family well-being, efficiency, social cohesion and integration, happiness, and so forth. To translate these into goals requires generating a priority list of preferred actions whereby both values and their calculated consequences are ranked in terms of preference, and the side effects of each are calculated and ranked in terms of preference.

The assumptions underlying the framework that sees policy as rational choice have been questioned on many grounds. For example, the information required to identify all policy alternatives and their consequences often is not available, nor are the resources for gathering or generating such information. Even if such information were available, Dye (1975) says, the likelihood that it would or could be used for decision making is questionable, given the diversity of values at stake on almost any given issue. Also, policymakers, like other people, have personal needs and deficiencies that may prevent them from conforming to rational decision-making norms. Uncertainties and ambiguities surrounding alternative courses of action serve only to exacerbate the problem, leading to the tendency to continue previously determined courses of action and thereby minimize the risk of unanticipated disruptive consequences.

Dye is not the only person to question the assumptions underlying this framework of policy choice. Herbert Simon (1957) in doing so raised the issue of limits on human capacity, particularly in relation to the complexity of the problems that confront policymakers. Problems, he said, often are so complex that attention to only a few of their aspects can be given at any one time. Such complexity produces segmented or factored problems, which precludes decision making that coordinates input from all specialists relevant to a decision. Simon developed the concept of "bounded rationality" to refer to the physical and psychological limits of a person's capacity to generate alternatives, process information, and solve problems. His work led him to conclude that rational action requires simple models dealing with the main features of a problem without capturing all of its complexity. Probably most collective real-world policy choices reflect a simplified version of the rational choice framework.

Policy as Incremental Choice

While policy as rational choice focuses attention on the formation of goals and strategies for achieving them, incrementalism focuses on the policy process itself (Frohock, 1979). Constrained by political considerations as well as those of time, money, and intelligence, policymakers are said to prefer ambiguity in articulating societal goals and in assessing "net value achievement" or the ratio of costs to benefits. First presented by Charles Lindblom (1959), incrementalism is regarded as a more accurate depiction of the policymaking process than rationalism in its pure form. Seen as structuring situations of choice in ways that constrain and confine it to relatively narrow limits, existing policies and programs as "outputs" become the frameworks through which policymakers come to understand and view problems that come to their attention. They provide the information policymakers use in making their decisions about problems. Also, having won their acceptance earlier, existing policies and programs enjoy a certain legitimacy that new policy and program proposals do not. Indeed, the preferences of policymakers for incremental choice is attributable both to the heavy investment in existing policies and programs and the uncertainties surrounding the consequences of adopting an entirely new or different set of policies and programs. Existing policies and programs also are more apt to continue because they represent gains and losses for affected groups. By the same token, because policy departures threaten to disrupt ongoing economic, organizational, and administrative processes and structures, and thus are likely to evoke dissensus and conflict, they are less likely to receive serious consideration.

If that policy is not made under conditions of natural harmony and effortless coordinated activity (Frohock, 1979), the process is complicated by the number of different people and motives that must be taken into account. In this regard, policymakers tend to act to satisfy constituent demands, and thus search for policy ideas and programs that seem most likely to work, not necessarily those that will work the best (Allison, 1971). Senator Moynihan's welfare reform proposal for families with children in poverty, which emphasizes the child support obligations of parents, mandatory education, training, or jobs, and public assistance to supplement parent earnings, reflects this. Herbert Simon (1957) refers to this phenomenon as "satisficing," finding a course of action that is good enough, a principle that substitutes for maximization. Under the principle of satisficing, the order in which alternatives are presented becomes critical since the search for them ends with the first alternative that is "good enough." Because incrementalism emphasizes short-run feedback procedures and relies on prompt corrective action, new considerations can be introduced into the process at any time and actions can be taken to correct deviations from desired outcomes relatively promptly. Within a context in which existing policies and programs are viewed as variations of past policies and programs, policy is viewed as a process of constant adjustment to the outcomes of previous action, an approach that incrementalists regard more favorably than the one based on predictions of future conditions, which can be only more or less accurate at best.

The important concepts that are a part of the framework that views policy as incremental choice are existing policies and programs as "outputs;" factored and segmented problems; uncertainty avoidance; satisficing; political feasibility; bounded rationality; goals as emergent rather than predetermined; sequential attention to goals; and short-term feedback. Policy as rational and incremental choice probably are the two frameworks that provide the most information about policy as substance because of the emphasis they place on values, goals, problems, and the historical-socioeconomic-political conditions from which problems emerge and require a policy solution. Developments pertaining to family policy are illustrative.

Policy as Rational Choice
Under Competitive Conditions

Policy as rational choice under competitive conditions refers to situations in which the outcomes depend on the choices and actions of two or more participants (Dye, 1975). Within this context, policymaking situations are perceived as a game in which the interdependent moves of relevant players determine the outcomes of the game. Such moves or choices reflect not only players' individual desires and abilities, but their expectations of the choices or moves of others as well. In order to predict the latter's moves and actions, such situations require each player to be aware not only of his or her own preferences, talents, and interests, but also those of his or her opponent(s) as well. Players can be individuals, groups, organizations at all levels, including governments— in short, any entity that has goals and is capable of rational action. The rules of the game define the choices available to players, including the possibility of bluffing and the deliberate misrepresentation of facts and attitudes. The payoff is what players receive as a result of their interdependent choices. Strategy, a key concept in game theory, refers to a set of moves designed to achieve the greatest payoff by taking into account all of the opponents' possible moves. Minimax is a strategy that attempts either to minimize maximum losses or maximize minimum gains, regardless of what the opponent does, its object being to protect the player against the opponent's best play. Rather than seeking maximum gains at the risk of greater losses, minimax seeks minimal gains as a protection against maximum losses.

Because cooperation is required to obtain desired outcomes in situations of conflict and competition, game theory concentrates on the tactics and strategies of individuals under conditions of no authority. As such, players are forced to bargain, negotiate, and compromise, and sometimes exchange side payments, or favors, to reach desired outcome. Players in competitive situations need not interact directly with each other, but instead may bargain with spectators, such as the electorate, to win support for their position, thus acting on the conditions that will help them secure the outcome they seek (Frohock, 1979). In this respect, game theory differs from power and control theories that include bargaining and negotiation among or between participants in direct interaction with each other. Allison (1971) advises that to understand and explain why a particular form of governmental decision was made, the observer must first identify the games and players, uncover the coalitions, bargains, and compromises, and appreciate the confusion of a process that includes moves that support a course of action, and also reflects the interests, power, and skill of individual participants.

Using game theory to guide his observations of bureaucracies, Allison (1971) summarized the nature of the policymaking situation as reflecting: (l) the existence of a diversity of goals and values that must be reconciled before a decision can be reached; (2) the presence of competing groups identified with alternative policies and goals within the official party leadership; and (3) differential group power. Differential group power is considered as important to the final decision as the appeal of the goals being sought, or the wisdom and cogency of the arguments. Policy from this perspective is viewed as a process of conflict and consensus building in which competition for support requires the use of persuasion, accommodation, and bargaining. The following list provides the concepts and constructs that are a part of the process Allison describes:

(1) actors as players in positions;
(2) actors' perceptions, characteristics, and personalities as influencing variables;
(3) the personal and organizational goals and interests of individual actors;
(4) the stakes of the game, which are the result of overlapping personal, organizational, and policy and program interests, and consideration of the welfare of others;
(5) deadlines and events that raise issues and force busy players to take stands on issues at appointed times;
(6) the effective influence of individual players, which is a blend of their bargaining advantages, their skill and will in using their advantages, and other players' perceptions of these two ingredients of influence; bargaining advantages stemming from formal authority, organizational position, control over resources, including information, and expertise that allow players to define the problem, identify the options, determine whether and in what form decisions are to be implemented; and their effectiveness and ability to affect other games—that is, their personal persuasiveness on positions and issues that have a high probability of being supported;
(7) action channels (which refer to the regularized means by which government takes action on specific issues and determines who the players are) that structure the game through the preselection of major players, and the distribution of the game's advantages and disadvantages;
(8) the rules of the game—from the Constitution, laws, court decisions, executive orders, conventions, and cultures—which define the

game, create the positions, distribute the power, and establish the procedures for taking action, and which sanction moves such as bargaining, coalition formation, persuasion, deceit, bluffs, and threats while defining others as illegal, unethical, or inappropriate;

(9) the action, which is the result not only of political processes in the context of shared power, but of individual judgments about important choices as well;

(10) the game—played in an environment that reflects uncertainty about what must be done, the necessity for doing something, and the critical consequences of what is done—the structure of the game and the confidence with which it is played, the rewards of the game with respect to influencing outcomes, and the game not being over once a decision is made inasmuch as decisions can be reversed or ignored.

A summary of the important concepts of this version of policy include: strategy, tactics, conflict, competition, cooperation, influence, power, negotiation and negotiating skill, bargaining, accommodation, persuasion, payoffs or rewards, compromises, actors as players in positions, stakes of the game, rules of the game, uncertainty, uncertainty avoidance, and policy as the outcome of the game. Perhaps one of the best examples of game theory in action as it pertains to family policy was the strategy Senator Helms employed when he used the filibuster to block the Reagan Administration's nomination of the ambassador to China because he objected to what he said was China's practice of coercive abortion and sterilization. Only after the administration agreed to withdraw its pledge of the final installment of $10 million to the United Nations Fund for Population Activities, which contributes money to China for its population control program, did he agree to support the administration's nomination.

Policy Choice as Equilibrium in Struggle Between Interest Groups

Interest group theory differs from game theory in that groups rather than individual players are seen to compete with each other for influence. Within this framework, individuals are important only when they act as a part of or on behalf of group interests. Thus the group is the mechanism through which individuals exert influence on government. An interest group comprises individuals who share similar views and interests around which they have organized for the purpose of making demands on government and influencing its decisions (Dye, 1975). Mothers Against Drunk Driving is an example. What distinguishes an interest group from other groups that also are organized around the shared interests of members is its political nature. A group becomes political if and when it makes a claim through or upon any of the institutions of government—at any level (Truman, 1971). Key determinants of group influence are membership size, wealth, organizational strength and cohesion, leadership, and access to decision makers. Changes in the relative influence of groups can be observed in changes in public policy, which tends to shift toward the interests of groups gaining in influence and away from those losing it. One example of such a shift is the diminished role of large city mayors in influencing urban policy to address the problems of minority families and families headed by women living in the central cities, which is a consequence of the expansion of suburbs and newer cities (Herbers, 1986).

Group theory holds that group struggle and conflict are descriptive of all meaningful political activity, that policymakers respond to demands and pressures from groups for government action in ways they each desire, policy choice being the equilibrium reached in the struggle among contending interest groups in their efforts to influence government action (Dye, 1975). Rules and procedures established by the political system serve to manage group conflict, as illustrated by the procedures used for the hearings that were held by the Governor's Council on Families and Children discussed in the previous chapter. The political system also manages group conflict by seeking to balance the interests of contending interest groups through compromise, arranging for and enacting and enforcing it. Within this context, policy is seen as the culmination of processes of negotiation, bargaining, and compromise among competing groups. Such compromise can be seen in the structure of government itself and the number of congressional committees representing the interests of particular groups that compete for their definition of the situation to prevail in choices affecting families. This process precludes the likelihood of there ever being a coherent approach to family policy in the United States, at least not in the very near future.

One strategy that politicians use to facilitate compromise is the formation of a majority coalition of groups, such as the coalition that sponsored the White House Conferences on Families. The main objective for forming coalitions is to mobilize and channel efforts toward achieving a goal or redressing a problem, such as the formation of the coalition to promote intergenerational equity or the coalition to mobilize action for housing for the homeless. The coalition of groups that form the New Right, which works to influence government action on such family issues as abortion, ERA, education, homosexuality, and pornography (Bohannon et al., 1983), is another example. In forming a coalition, the size of their constituency determines the latitude policy-makers have in selecting the groups to be represented in it and the diversity of interests it needs to represent. However, when its base is expanded to include widely diverse interests, the cohesion that may have helped to establish the coalition in the first place may be jeopardized (Zeigler and Huelshoff, 1980), the coalition that sponsored the 1980 White House Conferences on Families again being an example.

The maintenance of group equilibrium is made possible in a number of ways. One is through overlapping memberships by individuals who belong to more than one group. Overlapping memberships serve to moderate group demands because they involve areas of shared as well as conflicting interests. For example, individuals may simultaneously belong to a group that supports an increase in the minimum wage, but is opposed to sex education in the schools and another that supports sex education in the schools but opposes an increase in the minimum wage. Because groups seek to avoid offending members with multiple affiliations, they are prevented from moving too far from prevailing norms and values, or in a direction clearly opposite from that of others. Countervailing centers of power and influence in the United States also act to maintain group equilibrium in that no single group constitutes a majority, as does the structure of government institutions. Although the role of groups is to articulate demands and government's is to respond to them, the process can be reversed. Also, just as government develops policy proposals to which groups are invited to respond, groups with technical expertise also can develop such proposals (Ziegler and Huelshoff, 1980).

Within the interest group model, political parties are perceived as coalitions of interest groups and the political system an interest group system maintained in equilibrium by many forces. These include a large latent, almost universal, not generally visible group in American society that supports the Constitution and the ways in which the political system works (Dye, 1975). It is composed of people who tend to observe rather than participate in politics and are not likely to sustain participation in an organized interest group. In Mancur Olson's (1965) terms, they constitute a "potential group." An underlying assumption is that all groups have a common interest in maintaining the institutional framework within which group conflict occurs and, it is hoped, is resolved.

Key concepts and constructs of the interest group model are as follows: demands, politics as the struggle between competing groups; policy as the equilibrium reached among contesting interest groups; the group as individuals organized around shared interests and attitudes; group conflict, negotiation, bargaining, and compromise; coalitions; group influence as consisting of wealth, membership size, cohesion, leadership, access to decision makers; and so forth.

Policy Choice as Elite Preferences

While interest group theory directs attention to the influence of groups in making demands and in raising the issues for policymakers' attention, it views groups along lateral dimensions. In contrast, elite theory views groups and relationships vertically, and ranks them according to their effectiveness, prestige, wealth, size, and so forth. Thus elite theory draws attention to the hierarchical rankings of participating groups in accounting for family policy developments.

An underlying assumption of elite theory is that public policy does not reflect the demands of interest groups as much as it reflects the values and interests of elites (Dye, 1975; Frohock, 1979). In general, it is based on the assumption that the size and complexity of modern society and organizational life precludes the active and full participation of everyone in the political process, and that some division of labor is required to do the work of organized political life. Committees such as the Select House Subcommittee on Children, Youth, and Families that specialize in particular issue areas are the principle means by which such work gets done. Such committees are made up of representative members who constitute the *ruling or governing* elites. Ruling elites can be found in any organizational structure and in any political system and society, largely because of the absence of countervailing organized political interest and activity.

Allison (1971) describes the position of elites within a series of concentric circles consisting of (1) the general public or those who lie outside the circle because of their indifference to most policy issues; (2) the attentive public, which comprises the media, legislative bodies at different government levels, interest groups, and informed and inter-ested citizens who constitute the audience of government elites and are located one ring closer to center stage than the general public; (3) the policy and opinion elites who structure public discussion of issues and provide access or linkage to various social and political groups surrounding center stage; and (4) the real actors in the game, the official policy leadership, such as the president, governors, mayors, and their respective cabinets. Shaped by their positions within the structure, which in turn shapes their perceptions, the interests of government leaders often are competitive.

In general, elitism connotes consensus among elites about funda-mental norms and values underlying present institutional arrangements and the continuation of these institutions themselves. Elite consensus about fundamental values is considered essential for societal stability and survival. In the United States, elite consensus includes consti-tutional government, democratic procedures, majority rule, freedom of speech and press, freedom to form opposition parties and to run for public office, equality of opportunity, private property, individualism, and free enterprise, the values that underlie institutional structures and relationships. Thus from the vantage point of elitism, group competition centers around a very narrow range of issues. According to a survey undertaken of the attitudes of state legislators as governing elites toward family policy, general consensus exists that government should help families when necessary (Zimmerman et al., 1979). One stream of elite theory perceives elites as revolving; the other as fixed. The two views differ in the importance they attach to power (Dye, 1975). Traditionally, power is defined as a one-sided transaction between two or more actors in which the central action of the transaction is getting others to do something. The elite model, which views power as revolving and fluid, is based on the pluralistic nature of the American political system, and views elites as exercising power only within specialized areas and for a limited period of time. Thus its view of power is pluralistic, as being disbursed among a multiplicity of groups. To obtain the cooperation of other groups, the model emphasizes the importance of bargaining as a strategy for winning cooperation, and persuasion using standard face-to-face transactions when involving the general public. The fixed model of elite theory views power as being lodged in a single group over time, and is characterized less by an emphasis on negotiation and bargaining than by an emphasis on the manipulation of conditions and institutional arrangements in ways that favor that group's values and interests, as illustrated by the New Right. Such manipulation generally occurs without the knowledge of opposition groups, or direct face-to-face transactions with the general public, thus incorporating some of the elements of game theory.

Strategic elites refers to roles played by incumbents who possess information, make major decisions, especially with regard to alternative policies and strategies, and facilitate the implementation of these decisions. The actions of individuals in these roles are seen to be a function of the assumptions that are structured into these roles as well as those that they as individuals bring to them. For this reason, attention to the characteristics of persons who are strategic elites is critical. Advisers to presidents, governors, mayors, and executives of interest groups are among those who could be called strategic elites, as well as those without formal designation who provide information useful for policy choice. The importance of the characteristics of elites, strategic or governing, in the area of family policy is highlighted by the influence family life cycle stage was shown to have on the attitudes of legislators toward family policy in a survey of their attitudes toward family policy to which reference was made earlier (Zimmerman et al., 1979).

In general, elite theory incorporates many of the concepts associated with interest group theory. What is unique about elite theory is its ranking of groups in terms of their ability to influence the choice situation. Concepts such as fixed, revolving, governing, and strategic elites all direct attention to the different elites within a structure and the different roles they play in it.

Discussion and Conclusion

Frameworks for looking at policy as rational choice, as incremental choice, as the outcome of a competitive game, as the equilibrium reached among contesting interest groups, and as elite preferences each provide the concepts necessary for understanding family policy as both substance and process. Policy as rational and incremental choice probably lend themselves best to understanding the substance of individual family policies, while interest group, elite, and game perspectives lend themselves best to understanding the policy process and some of the factors that affect it. While no one framework can describe or explain all the phenomena relevant to policy choice as it relates to families, elements of all frameworks may be simultaneously operative in any given policy issue. One good example of this is welfare reform, which will be presented later in the book as a case study. But other examples abound: sex education in the schools, child care, parental leave, minimum wage, catastrophic health insurance, in-home health services, pay equity, child protection services, and so forth, all of which affect families directly, explicitly or implicitly.

To understand the linkages between policy and families requires an understanding, not just of policy as a course of action directed to the achievement of a goal or value and the factors that influence it, but of families themselves and different ways in which they can be understood. The next two chapters focus on different family frameworks that help provide such understandings. Because the systems framework conceptually is a linkage model and incorporates linkage as a concept, it will be used to link discussion of the policy frameworks in this chapter with discussion of the family frameworks that follow.

References

ALLISON, G. (1971) Essence of Decision: Explaining the Cuban Missile Crisis. Boston: Little, Brown.
BOHANNON, M., M. BUCKLEY, and E. OSBORNE (1983) The New Right in the States: The Groups, the Issues, and the Strategies. Conference on Alternative State and Local Policies, Washington, DC.
DYE, T. R. (1975) Understanding Public Policy. Englewood Cliffs, NJ: Prentice-Hall.
FROHOCK, F. (1979) Public Policy: Scope and Logic. Englewood Cliffs, NJ: Prentice-Hall.
HERBERS, J. (1986) "Mayors to mount effort to retain federal aid." The New York Times (March 9): 16Y.
LINDBLOM, C. (1959) "The science of muddling through." Public Administration Review 19: 79-88.
OLSON, M. (1965) The Logic of Collective Action: Public Goods and the Theory of Groups. Cambridge, MA: Harvard University Press.
SIMON, H. (1957) Models of Man. New York: John Wiley.
TRUMAN, D. (1971) The Governmental Process. New York: Knopf.
ZEIGLER, H. and M. HUELSHOFF (1980) "Interest groups and public policy." Policy Studies Journal 9, 3: 439-448.
ZIMMERMAN, S. L., P. MATTESSICH, and R. LEIK (1979) "Legislators' attitudes toward family policy." Journal of Marriage and the Family 41, 3: 507-518.

CHAPTER 5

Families as Social Systems: Implications for Family Policy

That policy can be viewed as the outcome of institutional arrangements, as rational choice, as incremental choice or variations of past policies and programs, as choice under competitive conditions, as the equilibrium reached among contending interest groups, or as elite preference says very little about the connections between policy and families, conceptually or practically. What are these connections? How can their family dimensions be highlighted to ensure their incorporation into all phases of the policy process—formulation, implementation, and evaluation—in order to protect this very important area of social reality from the untrammeled and often undesirable consequences of policies arising in other areas, as Myrdal (1968) has advised?

To do this requires some understanding of families beyond that which is conveyed in annual census reports and daily newspapers. Frameworks that have been applied to family phenomena and yield important insights into the connections between policy and families are the systems perspective, exchange and choice theories, symbolic interaction and family stress theory as a part of symbolic interaction, and conflict theory. Because the systems framework is so comprehensive in the concepts it offers and the abstractness of its concepts requires that they be elaborated, it alone is discussed in this chapter. The other frameworks will be presented together in Chapter 6.

Properties of Social Systems

According to Hill (1971), all social systems are characterized by four properties: (1) the tasks they perform to meet the needs and demands of their members and those of their environment; (2) the interrelatedness

- Task performance or functions
- Interdependence and interaction between and among component parts or relational networks
  - roles and positions
  - structural deficit
  - structural excess
- Boundary maintenance
  - open/closed systems
  - boundary permeability
  - liaison roles
- Equilibrium and adaptation
  - inputs, outputs
  - negative and positive feedback
  - information, energy, and material
  - mapping for variety
  - morpheostasis/morphogenesis
- Environment
  - general/specific
  - dynamic, interactive, and unpredictable

Figure 5.1   Systems Concepts

of positions or the interdependence of component parts that form their structures; (3) boundary maintenance tendencies that serve to differentiate systems from other social systems in their environment; and (4) equilibrium and adaptive propensities that tend to ensure their viability as social systems. Each of these properties will be discussed in conjunction with their elaborating concepts. The outline provided in Figure 5.1 acts as a guide to the discussion of framework.

Families as Social Systems: Their Tasks and Functions

The task-performing property of social systems pertains to the functions they are expected to perform. The primary functions families are expected to perform include: (1) physical maintenance and care of family members; (2) addition of new members through procreation or adoption and their relinquishment when they mature; (3) socialization of children for adult roles, such as those of spouse, parent, worker, neighbor, voter, and community member; (4) social control of members, which refers to the maintenance of order within the family and groups external to it; (5) production and consumption of goods and services needed to support and maintain the family unit; and (6) maintenance of family morale and motivation to ensure task performance both within the family and in other social groups. How families perform these tasks varies with ethnic and religious background, socioeconomic status, the age and sex of family members, the urgency of the tasks themselves, family life cycle stage, and the community and state in which they live. Tasks specific to family life cycle stages, such as the establishment stage, the childbearing stage, school age stage, adolescent stage, launching stage, postparental stage, and retirement stage, form the basis for family developmental tasks.

Although it is often asserted that the family has lost many of its basic functions to other institutions in society, evidence suggests that the family may be assuming more, not less, responsibility than in the past, if the implications of the demographic, political, and technological trends cited earlier are given due consideration. These include the increasing number of working mothers; the extension of life into far advanced years; the survival of those born with serious physical and mental defects who require ongoing family care; smaller families to share the care; deinstitutionalization policies that pertain to mentally ill, retarded, and physically disabled members; and cost-containment policies that restrict the availability of vital community services of all types, regardless of ability to pay (Zimmerman, 1978).

Interdependence of Family Roles

The concept of interdependence or interrelatedness of positions comprising a system refers to interacting and reciprocal positions and roles within a system's structure. Implicit in such positions are roles that must be performed if the family as a system is to fulfill its functions for its members and society. Through the interaction of actors in these positions—husband-wife, brother-sister, father-son, father-daughter, mother-son, and mother-daughter—a network of family relationships develops based on shared values and normative expectations that serve to unite the family and distinguish it from other groups. Even when members are geographically dispersed, families are able to retain their ties and family identity and participate in meaningful family exchanges as a result of modern systems of communication and rapid modes of transportation that enable them to visit and interact with one another frequently. Modern technology and banking systems facilitating arrangements for needed services for members in other communities when they become ill or disabled (Litwak, 1985) also contribute to maintenance of family ties. Although varying with culture and class, this relational network tends to continue until disrupted by the behaviors or one or more of its members who may challenge its values and norms, recruit others to it, or temporarily or permanently withdraw from it, psychologically, socially, and/or physically.

Because the family as a system functions with only a limited number of relatedness positions, tasks performed by members in positions they subsequently vacate must be assigned to those in the positions that remain (Hill, 1971). Reports of single parents indicate that remaining positions tend to become overburdened with too many tasks to perform. For this reason, family structures that have unoccupied positions are characterized as having a structural deficit. This is more serious for family task performance when it involves a parent or a spouse because of the greater leadership content in these positions.

Overburdened family positions may occur, not only because of a deficit in the family's structure, but because of new or additional tasks that families are expected to perform, such as the care of two sets of elderly parents in addition to a severely retarded child, two adolescents, and a disabled spouse. It also may occur when members themselves assume additional tasks, such as mothers who work outside the home or parents who work two jobs to make ends meet. Overburdened family positions may manifest themselves in family stress and disequilibrium as members try to cope with the multiple demands of their situation. Such stresses and strains can affect not only overall family task performance but also the performance of individual family members in their roles in other systems, such as school and work, threatening the viability of the family even further because of the interactive effects of different roles performed by the same individual member in different systems.

In contrast to structural deficit, an excess of structure may occur when too many members are available to fill family positions. This situation may occur in stepfamilies or in families with adult members sharing the same physical space or household. Indeed, the sharing of living space with parents and other family members already has become an alternative living arrangement for many young adults, as was noted earlier (U.S. Bureau of the Census, 1984). With increased longevity, this situation could extend to the grandparent generation as well. With regard to stepfamilies, dual problems of underfilled and overfilled positions often may be observed, underfilled for adults who are both parents and stepparents of two or more sets of children, and overfilled for children whose family position may be threatened by stepsibling competition. This could result in internal family conflict requiring outside intervention. In this regard, there is evidence to suggest that stepsibling relationships may be more conflictual than stepparent-child relationships (Marotz-Baden et al., 1979). Because of increased divorce rates, problems associated with structural deficit rather than excess have tended to predominate. However, with the increasing number of divorces involving an average of at least one child per divorce, and subsequent high rates of remarriage, the latter has become an increasingly prevalent situation among American families. According to the 1980 U.S. Bureau of the Census, the latest year for which these particular statistics were available, one of every eight children living with two parents lived with a natural parent and stepparent.

Boundary Maintenance

The boundary of any system may be conceptualized as the demarcation line that separates the system from its environment. It may be discerned through differences in the nature and intensity of patterns of interaction that take place within the system and between the system and its external environment (Katz and Kahn, 1966). Thus, in relation to families, the boundary pertains to patterns of interaction that differ in degree and kind from those that occur between families and such external organizations as schools, social service agencies, churches, workplaces, and so forth, in their external environment. The family as a semiclosed, semiopen system, is perceived to open selectively to engage in transactions with such organizations through liaison roles built into family positions (Hill, 1971), such as through children in their student role and parents in their roles as consumers, citizens, workers, service volunteers, interest group members, and PTA members. Because of the inevitability of intersystem linkages between families and their external environment, Sussman (1974) advises that families are required to train members for linkage competence. That confusion about boundaries can be problematic in the performance of linkage roles is evidenced by the paternity judge who fathered a child out of wedlock (Minneapolis Star and Tribune, 1986).

Because of the intimate functions the family performs for its members and the legal sanctions that can be imposed when its sanctity and privacy are threatened or invaded by outside intruders, the family as a boundary-maintaining system probably is more closed than other social systems. This is illustrated by the exclusion of parent-administered child discipline and corporal punishment in the proposed 1981 Family Protection Act's definition of child abuse. In this regard, it is of some interest to note that two characteristics that typify sexually abusive families is their highly closed nature as social systems and their confusion about subsystem parent-child and sibling boundaries.

Nevertheless, although the family often may exclude the outside world when coping with internal family problems, evidence suggests that as a system, the family may be more open than in the past and its boundaries more permeable. Members, for example, frequently seek the involvement of professionals outside the family, such as lawyers, psychotherapists, and family counselors, to help with internal family problems, or use outside support groups such as Parents Anonymous, Alcoholics Anonymous, or caregiver groups for this purpose. Changing norms and values in fact condone and often mandate penetration of family boundaries by government or government-regulated systems, child abuse laws, Baby Doe regulations, compulsory school attendance laws, and child support laws. Such laws and regulations may be desirable or undesirable in given situations, depending on their larger social purpose.

Equilibrium and Adaptation Propensities

The concepts of system equilibrium and adaptation involve several assumptions. The notion of equilibrium assumes a range of possible states within which the family as a system presumably can function and to which it can adapt (Hill, 1971). In terms of the family, if it develops patterns of interaction in conformity with the range of norms members share, it can survive as a system over time and space. The point at which this range has been exceeded becomes evident when one or more of its members withdraws from the family, as illustrated by runaway children or wives, or fathers who desert. Because of its variable size and rapidly changing age composition, the family could be more vulnerable to system instability than other organizations, given the adaptations it must make relative to roles, role expectations, role interdependencies, and patterns of family interaction over time. Whether or not this actually is so is an empirical question that would be interesting to examine.

NEGATIVE AND POSITIVE FEEDBACK PROCESSES

States of equilibrium and adaptation are made possible through negative and positive feedback processes that can be negative or positive in their consequences (Hill, 1971). To guide their functioning, social systems, regardless of the degree of their openness, use information from their external environment and internal component parts as well as feedback about their performance and to facilitate system self-awareness. Information and feedback incongruent with internally established goals are the basis for modifying system behaviors and operations, and are used as input into systemic decision-making processes. Thus families seek out and use information about changes in the social security program as input into decisions about retirement, and coordinate this information with other information pertinent to their income status. In this manner, they attempt to arrive at decisions that will ensure the viability of their economic functioning and the maintenance of family stability after they no longer derive their income from work.

To reduce the mismatch between information about a system's performance and its basic values, negative feedback processes begin to activate, triggering behaviors to bring about a convergence between the two when they diverge. Thus, with respect to families, information concerning increased interest rates may trigger actions to delay expenditures for such high-cost items as a home or car, just as in formation concerning decreased interest rates may trigger actions for their purchase. In this sense, negative feedback processes represent a change-resistant set of operations, geared toward system sameness, homeo- or morpheostasis, or the status quo, which in many situations may be desirable for effective system performance.

Positive feedback, on the other hand, is a deviation-amplifying rather than deviation-reducing process. Like negative feedback, it also begins with error or the mismatch of information about a system's behaviors relative to internal or external standards or criteria (Hill, 1971). Positive feedback processes are viewed as instructive and system enhancing, necessary for maintaining system viability, and essential to the mor-phogenic process through which systems grow and change. Examples of positive feedback in relation to families might be an adult daughter's defiance of her parent's wishes that she marry within the family's religion, or a housewife who informs her recalcitrant family of her decision to return to school, or a teenager who informs her white, middle-class parents that she is pregnant.

The morphogenic process by which systems grow and change can take many forms. It may take the form of a change in intercomponent relationships, such as parent/child relationships or spousal relation-ships, in the case of families, or a change in system values, purposes, and standards, as may occur in violent families after members engage in therapy, or in financially careless families after being threatened with bankruptcy. It also may take the form of a change in internal and external input operations, such as the increased influence of working wives in family decisions, or the entry of mothers with young children into the work force, or smaller size families. And finally, it may take the form of the ascendance of components with new and different properties and attributes in the governance and management of the system, as illustrated by families in which adolescents entering adult-hood are included in major family decisions.

Integrally related to the concepts of positive feedback and mor-phogenesis is the idea of "mapping for variety," and the necessity for a continuous flow of varied information, experience, and system input from the environment (Hill, 1971). Although mapping may reinforce what may be considered to be a desirable organizational state and hence result in homeostasis, in the case of families, positive feedback processes appear necessary to accommodate the changing needs of family members over the life span and the changing needs of the environment over time.

The Environment

The environment, according to Richard Hall (1972), consists of general conditions that apply to all systems as well as those that are specific to particular systems, such as families with disabled members. The general environment comprises broad technological, legal, eco-nomic, cultural, social, political, and ecological conditions affecting all systems, while the specific environment consists of conditions that are of immediate consequence to particular systems. Thus government constitutes the general environment of all families, while accessible, quality child care regulated by government standard setting agencies constitutes the specific environment of working parents with preschool children.

Noting the increasing importance of the environment for system performance, Terreberry (1972) characterizes the family's environment as turbulent, as presenting families with sudden unpredictable changes that continually threaten their equilibrium and undermine their adaptive capacities, often exceeding their ability to predict the future and thus control the compounding consequences of their actions. Thus the family as a system is vulnerable to disequilibrium, not only because of changes internally induced by members and its own developmental processes, but because of external environmental changes as well. Illustrative are sudden increases and decreases in the price of oil that affect the economic, social, and psychological functioning of millions of families, or the 1987 stock market crash, or the departure of long-established policy in government spending for goods, services, and jobs that families need. In this regard, Terreberry's (1972) conceptualization of the environment in terms of a focal organization's actual and potential transactional interdependencies is enlightening and useful since it connotes the dependence of the larger society on families as well as the family's dependence on society.

Implications for Family Policy

The concepts that the systems perspective provides—interaction, interdependence, tasks, roles, relational networks and their underlying norms and values, structural deficit and excess, boundaries and boundary maintenance, equilibrium and adaptation, negative and positive feedback, and environment—are important not only for viewing families in terms of structure, process, and function, but also for highlighting the nature of systemic relationships. The concept of transactional interdependencies about which Terreberry speaks relates to systemic exchanges that occur between systems through their respective input and output operations—families producing outputs as inputs for government, which in turn produces outputs as inputs for families. Both inputs and outputs refer to resources in the forms of information, money, and/or people. Thus family outputs may be expressed in the form of information about divorce rates, family poverty and homelessness, or members who are victims of AIDS, while government outputs may be expressed in the form of policies and programs that do or do not address family instability, poverty, and homelessness, or the needs of AIDS victims. While government outputs often are desirable inputs for families, this is not always the case. As a result, family outputs are not always desirable inputs for government or the larger society, or as has been said, "garbage in, garbage out."

In this regard, the relationship between the tasks that families perform and the tasks that government performs in the areas of health, education, income maintenance, social services, employment and manpower, and housing is useful to note: Education pertains to the socialization tasks of families; health to family procreation and the physical care of family members; income maintenance to family consumption and economic tasks; social services to the tasks of socialization, social control, and the maintenance or restoration of family morale; employment and manpower to the economic and production functions of families; and housing to the physical boundaries that define the space within which families perform their tasks, all of which are highly interrelated. Because of the special problems that poverty creates for the performance of family functions at all life cycle stages, how government performs its functions in these areas—that is, the nature of its outputs in these areas—is especially critical, given that the market cannot or does not meet certain needs or the needs of certain segments of the population. In this regard, the concept of structural deficit also is important since it implies that single-parent families may require additional social provision as structural supports in order to perform their functions effectively. The concept of over-burdened family positions similarly implies that families in overload situations also may require such social provision for the same purpose.

The concept of system linkages relates to system access and highlights not only the importance of socializing members to assume liaison roles, but also the importance of education and information about resources the community offers, the rules that govern their provision, and how to interact with members of other systems to negotiate access to them. This in turn has implications for the training and staffing of linkage positions in other systems. The concept of intersystem linkage also highlights the boundary issues implicit in policies that call for directly intervening in family systems, especially when such interventions represent the imposition of standards and values on families that may be incongruent with the beliefs and values of families of different religious or ethnic backgrounds.

The concept of the environment and environmental turbulence is related to family equilibrium and task performance. This relationship requires that outputs in the form of government policies contribute to environmental stability and not to environmental upset, and be more, rather than less, inclusive of families in all situations and at all life cycle stages, as a means of preventing family disequilibrium and breakdown. That a systems perspective views families in relation to their environment gives credence to policy strategies that aim to intervene in the environment to affect family conditions rather than those that aim to affect families only through direct interventions that invade their boundaries.

The comprehensiveness of the systems perspective, which makes it so appealing, can be overwhelming, especially because its concepts are so interrelated and abstract. For these very reasons, however, because of its very complexity and abstractness, it highlights aspects of the relationship between families and policies as government outputs in ways that no other framework can. Thus it is not too surprising that a systems perspective highlights the discrepancy that exists between the policy coherence that families systemically require and the fragmented, segmented collection of policies that existing structures and norms have produced. While all of the policy implications of a systems perspective related to families have hardly been drawn in this discussion, the concepts are there for future application. Also, although less comprehensive, other frameworks applied to the family provide useful ways for understanding the connections between families and policy that may be more comprehensible and thus easier to grasp and apply. These are presented in the next chapter.

References

HALL, R. (1972) Organizations: Structure and Process. Englewood Cliffs, NJ: Prentice-Hall.
HILL, R. (1971) "Modern systems theory and the family: a confrontation." Social Science Information 10: 7-26.
KATZ, D. and KAHN, R. L. (1966) The Social Psychology of Organizations. New York: John Wiley.

LITWAK, E. (1985) Helping the Elderly: The Complementary Roles of Informal and Formal Networks. New York: Guilford.

MAROTZ-BADEN, R., G. ADAMS, N. BUECHE, B. MUNRO, and G. MUNRO (1979) "Family form or family process? Reconsidering the deficit family model approach." Family Coordinator 28: 5-14.

Minneapolis Star and Tribune (1986) "Paternity judge named as father." (January 25): 2A.

MYRDAL, A. (1968) Nation and Family. Cambridge, MA: MIT Press.

SUSSMAN, M. [ed.] (1974) "Family, kinship, and bureaucracy," pp. 233-250 in Sourcebook on Marriage and the Family. Boston: Houghton Mifflin.

TERREBERRY, S. (1972) "The evolution of organizational environments," pp. 75-91 in K. Azumi and J. Hage (eds.) Organizational Systems. Lexington, MA: D. C. Heath.

U.S. Bureau of the Census (1984, March) Current Population Reports, Series P-20, No. 389, Marital Status and Living Arrangements. Washington, DC: Government Printing Office.

———(1980) American Families and Living Arrangements. Washington, DC: Government Printing Office.

ZIMMERMAN, S. L. (1978) "Reassessing the effects of public policy on family functioning." Social Casework 59, 8: 541-547.

CHAPTER 6

Other Family Frameworks and Their Implications for Family Policy

Other frameworks that have been applied to family phenomena that provide useful ways for understanding the connections between families and policy are exchange and choice theories (Blau, 1964; Ekeh, 1974; Gouldner, 1960; Heath, 1976; Levi-Strauss, 1966; Nye, 1979; Thibaut and Kelley, 1959), conflict theory (Coser, 1964; Dahrendorf, 1959; Deutsch, 1973; Levi-Strauss, 1966; Sprey, 1979); symbolic interaction (Burr et al., 1979; Mead, 1934; Stryker 1964); and family stress theory, which can be considered a part of symbolic interaction or by itself (Hill, 1949, 1958; McCubbin and Patterson, 1981). Although these frameworks are not as comprehensive as the systems framework in terms of the concepts they offer for interpreting the connections between families and policy, they are helpful in explaining why many policies often do not have the effects that policymakers and program planners had intended. The discussion will begin with exchange and choice theories.

Exchange and Choice Theories: Concepts and Assumptions

Among the basic assumptions underlying social exchange and choice theories are that families are made up of members, who as humans are rational and make decisions and initiate actions. Within the limits of the information they possess and their ability to predict the future, they make choices based on an assessment of the rewards and costs of various alternatives, choosing the one that seems to offer the greatest rewards for the least cost. To obtain such rewards, families incur costs by spending time and energy in engaging in one set of behaviors instead of another, foregoing the rewards of alternative choices. Unless no other promising alternatives are available and the costs are low, families will not repeat behaviors that have not been rewarded in the past. In other words, families seek to maximize rewards and minimize the costs of their behaviors and choices, although because rewards involve costs, potential rewards can be lost when costs are avoided.

REWARDS

Rewards are defined as pleasures, satisfactions, and gratifications that may be derived from particular statuses, relationships, interactions, and experiences. Rewards may include any of the following: (1) social approval, which includes respect, prestige, and admiration; (2) autonomy, which refers to the ability to choose activities, positions, relationships, and locales that offer high rewards entailing few costs; (3) physical security with respect to food, clothing, shelter, health care, physical safety, and so forth; (4) money that can be used to purchase goods and services; (5) agreement with one's values and opinions, or support for one's position, which psychologically reinforces feelings of self-worth and competence; and (6) equality in terms of what members can offer each other. For some, who think it adds interest to life and thus prevents boredom, ambiguity can be a source of reward; for others, because of the uncertainty it connotes it is a source of discomfort, and hence a cost.

Costs

Costs are defined as statuses, relationships, interactions, situations, or feelings that a family member regards as unpleasant, distasteful, or uncomfortable, and may take the form of rewards foregone as a consequence of choosing a competing alternative. Because the rewards and costs of alternative situations can never be completely known, and hence involve highly uncertain calculations, family members faced with alternative choices often experience considerable anxiety. Unpredictability, ambiguity, uncertainty, and anxiety all represent costs that family members must bear in situations that require choice, which often operate to prevent persons from seeking alternatives that may provide greater rewards than their present situation, status, or relationship. Illustrative are families of an unemployed breadwinner faced with the choice of moving to another community to search for a job or remaining in the community in which they live in hopes that one will emerge. Battered wives fearful of leaving their spouse because they are unsure they can "go it alone" also are illustrative.

PROFITABILITY

The profitability of an alternative choice can be determined by assessing the rewards and costs of a contemplated sequence of actions. Thus, in choosing an alternative, the potential for a more profitable outcome must be such that the choice absorbs the uncertainty it creates and also compensates for it. From this perspective, the choice of a divorced mother to remain on AFDC instead of taking a low-paying job of uncertain duration with few benefits or opportunities for upward mobility is understandable in light of the economic security AFDC offers, however inadequate the benefits. Perceptions vary, however, with respect to rewards and costs and the balance between them, choices reflecting values that families assign to relationships, statuses, experiences, and objects. By noting their choices, and asking them what they like and do not like, and observing their behaviors, the relative costs and rewards of given situations for families can be determined by an outside observer.

COMPARISON LEVEL AND
COMPARISON LEVEL ALTERNATIVES

Comparison level is another concept encompassed in exchange and choice theory frameworks that is helpful for understanding how families might perceive and experience policy. According to Thibaut and Kelley (1959), comparison level is a standard by which families evaluate the rewards and costs of their situation in relation to what they think it should be. Those who perceive they are less well off than they deserve will feel angry and those who perceive that they are better off than they deserve will feel guilty, anger and guilt both representing costs. Individuals and families make such comparisons intuitively; computer simulations often are used to compare outcomes for aggregates of families. The comparative analyses of the effects of different tax plans for families in different income groups undertaken during the 1986 congressional tax reform debate are illustrative. The concept of comparison level alternatives is defined as the comparison of outcomes of alternative situations, relationships, or statuses in terms of their rewards and costs (Thibaut and Kelley, 1959), such as the rewards and costs of paying more or less taxes for individual families.

RECIPROCITY

The assumptions that underlie these frameworks apply to relationships not only within and between families, but can also apply to the relationship between families and policy as well. Because families are capable of anticipating greater rewards and fewer costs when government institutions are responsive to needs, they pay taxes and often expend considerable time and energy in trying to improve government policies and programs (Nye, 1979). In return, they anticipate better health, greater economic security, and an improved quality of life as rewards that are widely shared. Based on the principle of reciprocity, they also recognize that the alternatives they choose affect the rewards and costs that others may anticipate as well, compliance with no smoking ordinances and the 55 mile per hour speed limits being examples.

In exchange and choice theories, the principal of reciprocity takes precedence over the principal of profitability, or of striving for the most favorable reward/cost ratio (Nye, 1979). Reciprocity implies interdependence, a spirit of mutuality, of taking other people into account in making choices, and is based on the assumption that people should help, not hurt, others, especially those who have helped them in the past.

Thus the concepts that are central to exchange and choice theories—costs, rewards, comparison levels, comparison level alternatives, satisfaction, profitability, and reciprocity—offer important clues for considering the implications of policies for families and their members and how such implications might vary according to family socioeconomic status, ethnic and religious background, family life cycle stage, and so forth, and with the particular issue at hand.

Conflict Theory: Concepts and Assumptions

Another conceptual framework that has been applied to the family and extended to better understand the relationship between families and policy is conflict theory—for two rather contradictory reasons. One is that the relationship between families and government is perceived by some as adversarial. At the same time, government, via the courts, is often called upon to resolve conflict within and between families, and between families and formal organizations, such as industrial firms, insurance companies, retail stores, schools, social agencies, and hospitals.

COMPETITION

One of the assumptions underlying conflict theory is that within any given system, conditions of scarcity exist to create a competitive zero-sum structure such that gains for one member constitute losses for others. It further assumes that situations are structured in ways that allow members to gain at one another's expense or win or lose as a group. However, despite their complex structure of competitive relationships, groups also are symbiotic in nature, and thus come together because of the common bond and joint needs of members. Such symbiosis simultaneously reduces and minimizes the rewards of competition, and accounts for the willingness of members to cooperate and compromise on matters of dispute, not always understanding what is at stake. Conflict arises over scarce resources, whatever the issue.

Conflict, like competition, can arise among members of a family, or between families and other organizations, or the larger society over any number of issues—abortion, school prayer, school dress codes, child discipline or socialization, the treatment of defective newborns, euthanasia, and so forth. Conflict can take a variety of forms, ranging from the physical abuse of one family member by another, the bombing of family planning clinics, and neighborhood harassment of individual families, to court litigation.

CONFLICT RESOLUTION

To bring an end to conflict, a solution must be found that the respective parties will acknowledge and accept, even when the underlying competitive structure of their relationship remains. One of the ways conflict can be resolved in a competitive situation is through its redefinition or restructuring to enable those involved to better manage it. To completely eliminate competition among contending parties, however, requires that one be removed from the situation. Many child custody cases are of this nature. Also illustrative is the famous Baby M case in which the surrogate mother was artificially inseminated by Baby M's father because of the risk that pregnancy posed for his wife. Because the surrogate mother refused to relinquish the baby to the baby's father and wife as had been agreed, the case was brought to court to resolve the conflict.

PERSUASION, NEGOTIATION, BARGAINING

Persuasion is considered a more appropriate means of resolving conflict than the creation of a win-lose situation when differences arise among those who share similar views and knowledge about the world. Persuasion suggests that the opposing party has been brought to accept the other's point of view. Negotiations and bargaining, which are likely to precede overt conflict among contesting parties, sometimes occur concurrently with it and are associated with its termination. Negotiation is an exchange process designed to reach collective agreement on an issue of dispute among parties, as when family members attempt to negotiate fees with their physicians or accountants. Negotiation includes all forms of bargaining, although in bargaining, participants who generally view themselves in an adversarial relationship to one another try to gain personal advantage for themselves over others. Negotiation, bargaining, and conflict all represent continuing attempts to influence the direction and outcomes of contested events or decisions. When many conflicting interests are at stake, rules are necessary to protect the interests of everyone concerned, although rules themselves can involve considerable conflict.

POWER, AUTHORITY AND PRIVILEGE

Power, on the other hand, connotes the ability effectively to control the situation, whether this involves people, information, service, or material goods, and the potential to control the direction or outcome of a joint course of action by demanding compliance, which often cannot be determined until negotiated outcomes are known. Power in essence describes the relationship between government and families in certain areas, such as taxes and child protection. A resource in most institutionalized relationships, power can be viewed in terms of either authority or privilege. Power and authority are implicit in the parent-child relationship, employer-employee relationship, doctor-patient relationship, probation officer-probationer relationship and so forth.

Authority based on the power associated with position connotes a hierarchical relationship among members. Privilege, on the other hand, is defined as a competitive advantage that some members of a system have that others do not. It may be associated with position, but it also may reflect special access to scarce resources, such as information or money. Cases of contested privilege have involved leaves of absence for all pregnant women who request them, with employers arguing that such leaves are discriminatory in that they treat one class of worker different from others, and conflict with federal laws prohibiting discrimination on grounds of pregnancy alone.

CONFRONTATION AND APPEASEMENT, THREATS AND PROMISES

Conflict also can involve both confrontation and appeasement, either of which can be constructive or destructive in their consequences. Aggressive, assertive behavior is aimed at getting others to behave in the manner the aggressor desires. It occurs at the expense of others and takes the form of punishment or deprivation when the aggressors' demands are not met, a description that fits most abusive family situations. Although promises resemble threats structurally in that both are coercive, promises are different from threats in that the latter conveys some type of punishment, while the former is regarded as a constructive positive reinforcer. Both rely on shared understandings for their effectiveness.

Conflict theory provides not only the conceptual tools for understanding the nature of many of the connections between families and policy, but also the tools for acting on such understandings: negotiation, bargaining, compromise, persuasion to effect a better connection between families and policy. Marital rape laws, child custody rulings, surrogate parent rulings, the expansion of marital property to include the education of a spouse in divorce settlements, medical malpractice suits, and so forth are all examples of conflict situations that join families and policy, judicially, administratively, and legislatively. Many others could be cited.

Symbolic Interaction: Concepts and Assumptions

In general, symbolic interaction has not been considered an appropriate framework for analyzing the relationship between families and policy. In part, this is because its application to families has tended to focus inward on interactions within the family unit. Yet many of the concepts that are central to this framework provide useful insights for understanding the relationship between families and policy. Dealing with subjective experience within the context of "objective reality," symbolic interaction provides a way for understanding the subjective and interpersonal aspects of family policy.

SOCIALIZATION

Symbolic interaction focuses on the problem of the individual in relation to society in terms of socialization and personality organization (Stryker, 1964). Socialization refers to the process by which the individual acquires characteristic ways of behaving, and the values, norms, and attitudes of the social groups of which he or she is a part. These groups include families and other institutions such as day-care centers, schools, churches and synagogues, youth serving groups, work settings, voluntary organizations, and associations of all kinds, including political parties, all of which perform a socialization function. Socialization refers to developmental processes and that which happens over time. With respect to personality organization, which refers to persistent patterns of behavior, symbolic interaction limits its considerations to that which falls within the normal range. Thus it represents a departure from psychological theories that focus on personality pathology.

ROLE AND ITS DERIVATIVES

One of the important concepts of symbolic interaction relevant to this discussion is role and all of its derivatives: role performance, role enactment, role behavior, role competence, role ambiguity, role consensus and dissensus, role expectations, role location, role compatibility or congruence of the role with self, role rewards, and role strain. Role is defined as relatively integrated sets of distinguishable social norms (Stryker, 1964) or expectations concerning behaviors appropriate to it. Role also refers to behavior associated with positions or statuses in social structures, such as father, mother, daughter, son, grandparent, sibling, and so forth. For this reason it is said that people tend to view their social situation as a set of statuses and roles. Although roles by definition always consist of socially shared expectations, how they are enacted is seen to emerge through interactional processes; hence they are dynamic as well as prescribed. Thus some latitude exists for personal and situational differences when roles are enacted and performed, although when performance departs too far from acceptable norms, conflict among family members and between families and the larger society may arise.

One of the ways in which people learn roles is through anticipatory socialization, which refers to the process of learning about norms, values, attitudes, and other dimensions of a role before assuming it. Anticipatory socialization is thought to ease role transitions, which often involve role strain and conflict, particularly for roles assumed for the first time without formal preparation. Examples include an expectant first-time mother learning the essentials of infant care prior to the infant's birth, or persons learning the skills of a job they would like to have, or unemployed persons attending a workshop on how to look for a job.

DEFINITION OF THE SITUATION

Another concept central to symbolic interaction that is relevant to this discussion is definition of the situation, which refers to the perceptions and subjective meanings of a situation for families. A situation is defined as a number of stimuli that relate to each other in a special way in acting on families and their members. Symbolic interaction is based on the assumption that people live in a symbolic as well as physical environment and acquire complex sets of symbols in their minds or cognitive frameworks (Burr et al., 1979). While many symbols such as the Moral Majority or the "war on poverty" or "welfare," are linguistic, they also may be auditory, or visual. The meanings that attach to such symbols are cultural; people decide what and what not to do based on the symbols they have learned in their interactions with others and their beliefs about the importance of a symbol's meanings. The proposition that the definition of a situation influences its effects such that the latter tends to be congruent with the definition has special meaning for family policy, as evidenced when the federal government attempted to redefine poverty to change perceptions about its prevalence and thereby justify policy neglect of the problem (Schorr, 1984).

SATISFACTION AND RELATIVE DEPRIVATION

Also incorporated within the framework of symbolic interaction is the concept of satisfaction. Satisfaction refers to a subjectively experienced phenomenon of pleasure, contentment, and/or happiness. It also has been defined as a condition of congruence between expectations and rewards that is conceptually related to the concept of comparison level, a part of exchange and choice theories. Relative deprivation, another concept conveying the idea that how people evaluate their situation is partly a function of how they view it in relation to significant others, groups, and/or points of comparison in their lives, similarly is conceptually related to comparison level. Like comparison level, relative deprivation does much to explain dissatisfaction among families when comparing their situation to that of others, particularly when differences are attributable to policy choices giving one group of families an advantage but not others.

Particularly relevant in terms of this discussion are the summary statements of some of the contributors to symbolic interaction: that individuals and society are two sides of the same phenomena, each being dependent on the other (Cooley, 1902); that if people define a situation as real, it is real in its consequence (Thomas and Thomas, 1928); and that interaction as a principle of social life applies not only to internal family relationships but also to the relationship between the family and its environment (Burgess, 1926). Through such interaction, Burgess said, the family forms a conception of itself, and becomes a unit with ties to the community and the larger society. Indeed, because the concepts of symbolic interaction have not been applied to the understanding of the connections between families and policy, analysis of their connections has suffered accordingly. Many so-called policy failures might have been anticipated had some consideration been given to how affected families perceived and defined their situation, the meanings they attached to particular policies and programs, and their statuses and roles in relation to them. Many policies would benefit from an understanding of the subjective as well as the objective aspects of policy as it is experienced by families and their members, as will be illustrated in two of the case studies presented in this book.

Family Stress Theory: Concepts and Assumptions

Although the family stress framework could be discussed within the framework of symbolic interaction because of the concepts it employs, the term *family stress* is of such common reference that it is being discussed separately from, although in relation to, symbolic interaction.

Like the other frameworks, it too offers concepts useful for thinking about the connections between families and policy.

Hill's original crisis model begins with A, the stressor event, interacting with B, the family's crisis meeting resources, interacting with C, the family's definition of the situation, which may lead to X, the crisis situation (Hill, 1949, 1958). These are the central concepts of the framework. The stressor event, the A factor, is considered to be the factor that creates or induces family change. In the vocabulary of family scientists, such events may be normative and/or non-normative, the former referring to expectable, taken-for-granted events in the life cycle of the family, and the latter to unexpectable life events. Examples of the former include marriage, the birth of a child, the child's entry into school, and so forth, which are of a different order than such non-normative life events as a tornado, a fire, a car accident, or the winning of a million dollars. Both the normative and non-normative can manifest themselves in a single event, as illustrated by the birth of a severely handicapped infant. Whether normative or non-normative, stressor events involve changes in patterns of family interaction, family boundaries, family goals, roles, and/or values. Such changes may be viewed as demands the family is required to meet. Demands have the potential for upsetting the balance necessary for effective family functioning, depending on the family's resources.

The B factor, family resources, includes family integration, which refers to a characteristic that develops out of common interests, shared values, mutual affection, financial interdependence, and family adaptability, which refers to the ability to overcome difficulties and change direction (Olson et al., 1979). Other resources might include agreement among family members as to roles, the primacy of family goals and needs relative to personal goals; and satisfactions the family as a unit derives from meeting the needs of members and moving toward its collective goals (Cavan and Ranck, 1938; Koos, 1946). Also of critical importance are resources such as the psychological and physical health of family members; a family structure organized to meet the needs and demands of members effectively; time, energy, money, negotiating skills, knowledge and information, friends, and community. Whatever the resources, however, they must be appropriate to the demands of the situation and what the situation requires to maintain the necessary demand/resource balance for individual families.

The C factor represents the family's subjective perceptions of the situation, the factor that is integral to the symbolic interaction orientation. Such perceptions reflect the family's values and previous experience in dealing with change and in meeting unfamiliar situational demands, whether their source is external or internal to the family. The X factor, the crisis, refers to the incapacity rendered to the family by the stressor event. If the family does not perceive and define the situation as a crisis and has the resources for meeting the demands of the situation created by the event, it may never experience a crisis. The Double ABCX model developed by McCubbin and Patterson (1981) takes a longitudinal perspective with respect to family stress and crisis by extending the original ABCX model over time. According to these researchers, the course of family adaptation relative to a stressor event appears to be influenced by four additional factors: (1) additional stressors, or stress pile-up, the aa factor; (2) family efforts to generate new or additional resources to bring to bear on the situation, the bb factor; (3) modifications in family perceptions and views of its entire situation, the cc factor; and (4) family coping strategies that facilitate adjustments and adaptations to the situation. In a different formulation, coping strategies might be viewed as a bb factor—or an aa factor— since particular coping strategies, such as alcohol abuse, would contribute to existing family strains and tensions, and hence be an added stressor, while other coping strategies, such as therapy or volunteer work, might alleviate them, and hence be an added resource. External demands or stressors may take a variety of forms, including the curtailment of services resulting from cutbacks in government programs upon which many families have depended. Further, because families and individuals are not static but change over time, the nature of the demands they experience can be expected to change accordingly.

The important concepts in the family stress framework, whether they pertain to the single or Double ABCX model are: demands or stressors, normative and non-normative life events, the family's crisis-meeting resources, the family's perception and definition of its situation, and the crisis situation. To these, the Double ABCX model adds the concept of coping strategies and a longitudinal perspective. Because stressors and resources pertain to external as well as internal sources, they have particular relevance for thinking about the connections between families and policy: When does policy act as a stressor and when does it act as a resource for families, for which families, and to what degree? Can the resource aspects of policy be strengthened when it is formulated?

Discussion and Conclusion

Although the separate frameworks relate to one another in different ways, and the meanings of some of their concepts are similar, the pattern in which the concepts are arranged are different. Thus while exchange and choice theories talk about costs and rewards, stress theory talks about stressors and resources, and conflict theory about wins and losses. Definition of the situation, which is central to symbolic interaction, also is important to family stress theory, conflict theory, and to the family systems perspective. Values, on the other hand, play a more important role in exchange and choice theory since they determine what constitutes costs and rewards. The idea of relative deprivation and satisfaction, which are a part of symbolic interaction, are very similar in meaning to comparison level and comparison level alternative in exchange and choice theory, all of which call attention to the comparative evaluations families make of their situation. The idea of reciprocity carries a connotation similar to that of interdependence in the systems perspective, and also symbiosis in conflict theory; more important is the meaning it connotes for the relationship between families and government and policy as output. Role and all of its derivatives have significance for family policy since so much of it is concerned with roles, role performance, and statuses. In this regard, stressors, demands, resources, and pile-up from family stress theory also have special meaning for family policy.

Thus if policy were to be designed from a family perspective using exchange and choice theories, consideration would be given to the costs and rewards such policy involves for families. In the case of teen pregnancy, for example, policies would be designed to improve the life conditions of poor teenagers through education and jobs to make the costs of pregnancy higher. If policy were to be designed from a family perspective using conflict theory, strategies would be designed to ensure fair outcomes for those in less powerful positions in contested situations, whether the latter involves other family members or families and societal institutions. From the vantage point of symbolic interaction, policy from a family perspective would be designed to increase satisfactions, take family definitions of the situation into account as a way of anticipating their responses. Policy from the perspective of family stress theory would be designed to increase the resources available to families, reduce the demands so that families could maintain their equilibrium and continue to carry out their institutional and systemic functions. Many of the problems and issues with which family policy is concerned—teen pregnancy, abortion, poverty, homelessness, education, health care, maternity and parent leaves, child support, long-term care, and so forth—could be better understood from a family perspective through one of these conceptual frameworks. The relevance of the family systems framework, choice and exchange theories, and family stress theory for policy will be illustrated in the case studies that follow. Because three are based on research, each case illustrates not only the connection between families and policy from a family perspective, but the connection between policy and research as well. The case of welfare reform will be treated somewhat differently in that it will be approached from the vantage point of policy choice that integrates all of the policy frameworks and incorporates a family perspective.

References

BLAU, P. M. (1964) Exchange and Power in Social Life. New York: John Wiley.

BURGESS, E. W. (1926) "The family as a unity of interacting personalities." Family 7: 3-9.

BURR, W. R., G. K. LEIGH, R. D. DAY, and J. CONSTANTINE (1979) "Symbolic interaction and the family," pp. 42-111 in W. R. Burr et al. (eds.) Contemporary Theories about the Family, Vol. 2. New York: Free Press.

CAVAN, R. and K. R. RANCK (1938) The Family and the Depression. Chicago: University of Chicago Press.

COOLEY, C. H. (1902) Human Nature and the Social Order. New York: Scribner's.

COSER, L. A. (1964) The Functions of Social Conflict. New York: Free Press.

DAHRENDORF, R. (1959) Class and Conflict in Industrial Society. Stanford, CA: Stanford University Press.

DEUTSCH, M. (1973) The Resolution of Conflict. New Haven, CN: Yale University Press.

EKEH, P. (1974) Social Exchange Theory. Cambridge, MA: Harvard University Press.

GOULDNER, A. W. (1960) "The norm of reciprocity." American Sociological Review 25: 161-178.

HEATH, A. (1976) Rational Choice and Social Exchange. Cambridge, England: Cambridge University Press.

HILL, R. (1958) "Generic features of families under stress." Social Casework 49: 139-150.

———(1949) Families Under Stress. New York: Harper.

KOOS, E. L. (1946) Families in Trouble. New York: Kings Crown Press.

LEVI-STRAUSS, C. (1966) "The bear and the barber." Journal of the Royal Anthropological Institute 93: 1-11.

McCUBBIN, H. I. and J. M. PATTERSON (1981) Systematic Assessment of Family Stress, Resources, and Coping: Tools for Research, Education, and Clinical Intervention. Family Social Science, Family Stress Project. St. Paul: University of Minnesota.

MEAD, G. H. (1934) Mind, Self and Society. Chicago: University of Chicago Press.

NYE, F. I. (1979) "Choice, exchange, and the family," pp. 1-41 in W. Burr et al. (eds.) Contemporary Theories about the Family, Vol. 2. New York: Free Press.

OLSON, D. H., D. H. SPRENKLE, and C. S. RUSSELL (1979) "Circumplex model of marital and family systems: cohesion and adaptability dimensions, family types, and clinical application." Family Process 18: 3-27.

SCHORR, A. L. (1984) "Change the definition in poverty decline." Minnesota Star and Tribune (May 18): 25A.

SPREY, J. (1979) "Conflict theory and the study of marriage and the family," pp. 130-159 in W. Burr et al. (eds.) Contemporary Theories about the Family, Vol. 2. New York: Free Press.

STRYKER, S. (1964) "The interactional and situational approaches," pp. 125-170 in H. Christensen (ed.) Handbook of Marriage and the Family. Chicago: Rand McNally.

THIBAUT, J. W. and H. H. KELLY (1959) The Social Psychology of Groups. New York: John Wiley.

THOMAS, W. I. and D. S. THOMAS (1928) The Child in America. New York: Knopf.

PART III
APPLICATIONS OF FRAMEWORKS TO FAMILY POLICIES

CHAPTER 7

Welfare Reform as a Case of Family Policy

Welfare and welfare reform have been on and off the public agenda for at least the last two decades. They are topics that involve complex economic, psychological, political, social, cultural, family, ethical, and moral issues about which people evidence very strong feelings. The primary purpose of this chapter is not to provide a detailed review of the history of welfare reform, but rather to use it to illustrate family policy as content and process. The present discussion begins with the debates that took place in the late 1960s and early 1970s concerning alternative proposals "to reform the welfare system." These debates are examples of policy as rational choice in terms of the consideration of alternative courses of action for dealing with the problem of welfare and assessments of their consequences for the value goals they each maximized. The actions that actually followed, however, are better examples of policy as incremental choice. Because of their timeliness, alternative proposals "to reform the welfare system" in the 1980s are included in the discussion, which not only says something about the unfinished nature of policy business but about welfare reform in particular. The chapter concludes with a brief discussion that suggests how welfare reform might be viewed from a family perspective, drawing on the family frameworks that were presented in the previous two chapters.

Brief Historical Background of AFDC

The term *welfare* properly refers to all programs based on need, such as food stamps, Medicaid, state supplementary income programs for elderly, blind, and disabled persons, subsidized housing, student loans, and so forth. More broadly, it applies to all government subsidized programs, such as farm aid, community development programs, small business programs, highway construction, foreign aid, and so forth. However, in this discussion when reference is made to welfare and welfare reform, it is in relation to Aid to Families with Dependent Children (AFDC) and proposals for its revamping. AFDC is a financial assistance program for families with dependent children in which the primary breadwinner is absent from the home or, as in 25 states, is unemployed. AFDC began with the Social Security Act in 1935 as a protection, President Franklin Roosevelt said, against misfortunes that "cannot be wholly eliminated in this manmade world of ours." In this regard, it represented a break from traditional institutional arrangements in that for the first time the federal government joined states and localities in accepting responsibility for the economic support of children whose fathers were absent from the home because of death or desertion (Ross, 1985). Originally called ADC (Aid to Dependent Children), its forerunner was the widow's pension law that states first enacted in 1911 to provide financial assistance to widowed mothers to enable them to care for their children in their own home, spreading to all but two states by 1935. Prior to the widow's pension law, indigent children and adults were placed out of the home to work in the homes of other families in exchange for bed and board; if unable to work, they stayed in alms or poorhouses.

ADC was conceived as a small residual means tested program to protect a small number of female-headed families not covered by other income maintenance programs, such as the social insurance retirement program, the unemployment insurance program, and the workmen's compensation program, which were all work related (Schorr, 1966). The theory was that the need for means tested public assistance programs such as AFDC, OAA, AB, and AD (Old Age Assistance, Aid to the Blind, and Aid to the Disabled), which also were developed as part of the Social Security Act, would diminish as the economy recovered since all workers and their dependents, and hence almost everyone, eventually would be covered by social security (Moynihan, 1968). Unlike social security, which is financed by employer-employee contributions and designed to meet the economic needs of workers whose earnings have been interrupted because of retirement or old age, temporary unemployment, or disability, AFDC is financed by federal, state, and local governments out of general revenues through taxes.

That AFDC did not wither away as was originally envisioned reflects many of the realities to which reference was made earlier: increasing numbers of families with dependent children headed by divorced, separated, or never married women, the failure of many noncustodial fathers to meet child support obligations; mothers' lack of skills, education, or experience necessary for competitive employment; their lack of access to affordable, quality day care, or transportation to seek and retain a job; an occupational structure that confines minorities and women to low-paying, unstable jobs that offer few benefits such as health insurance; and a no- or slow-growth economy that cannot provide enough jobs on a consistent continuing basis at wages high enough to support a family. For blacks, the situation was and is worse both because of racial discrimination and their lack of preparation for competing in the labor force in the wake of the agricultural revolution in the South that forced them off the land. Also, the transformation of many public programs into entitlements that citizens could claim as a legal right in the wake of the rights revolution of the late 1960s and early 1970s meant not only that AFDC was not going to wither away, but that in fact it was destined to grow for a time. In 1985 AFDC provided benefits for 3.7 million families with 7 million children (Social Security Bulletin, 1987).

In the 1960s, the civil rights movement and the War on Poverty brought the deficiencies of existing programs, especially AFDC, to the fore. AFDC came under widespread attack on grounds that it was inequitable, inefficient, inadequate, fiscally burdensome, a violation of human rights, antiwork, antifamily, and so forth. More specifically, families in similar circumstances were treated differently in different states and counties within states. Many states did and still do not provide benefits that meet their own needs standards. A marginal tax rate of 100% on earnings in effect penalized mothers for working, reducing their monthly benefits by one dollar for every dollar they earned, creating a disincentive for them to work. The means test, which is a declaration of poverty and one of the requirements for AFDC eligibility, was experienced as demeaning and stigmatizing. Unannounced midnight raids in search of a man in the house to ensure compliance with the program's absent father requirement violated mothers' privacy rights. Residency requirements restricting the mobility that families needed to improve their situation also violated their civil rights. Fathers were and in 25 states still are required to be absent from the home, "tearing families apart." The program's federal-state-county financing and administration was and is complex and economically and administratively inefficient. A source of conflict between workers and clients and clients and nonclients, it was viewed as socially divisive. Conservatives complained and continue to complain about how costly the program is, creating a drain on the public treasury. By providing income not derived from work, they said it encouraged personal slothfulness and laziness, which obstructed the operations of the free market and its requirements for productivity and efficiency.   It was within this context that President Johnson stimulated the search for alternatives to AFDC and other public assistance programs to reduce the incidence of poverty and close the poverty gap, which it was estimated would require $15 billion (Garfinkle, 1983). In light of the anticipated surplus in the federal budget in 1968, the sum was small enough to make this goal seem feasible (Brazer, 1968), giving contextual reality to the debates about alternatives to welfare.

Alternatives to AFDC: The Negative Income Tax

The two major alternative approaches to AFDC and other public assistance programs that were discussed at the time were children's allowances (CA) and the negative income tax (NIT). The negative income tax and guaranteed annual income often were regarded as synonymous, but like children's allowances, NIT is only one form of a guaranteed annual income. A guaranteed annual income refers to a basic minimum income that is guaranteed by the federal government. It may take the form of a negative income tax, children's allowances, unemployment insurance, jobs, or income insurance such as McGovern proposed in 1972.

The negative income tax refers to a cash payment by the federal government to individual families that partially or wholly subsidizes a family's income up to a specified minimum income level based on a preestablished formula that takes family size and income into account. The basic components of a negative income tax program are the break-even point, the marginal tax rate, and the minimum benefit level. The break-even point refers to the point at which the person becomes liable for tax payments to the government, prior to which the government is liable for income payments to the individual, which is the negative income tax. The marginal tax rate refers to the rate at which earned income is taxed, which may be anywhere from 20% to 50%, or in the case of AFDC under the more recent rules, 100%. The minimum benefit level refers to the basic minimum benefit guarantee to which an individual or family having no other income would be entitled.

Although plans differed with respect to their break-even points, benefit levels, and marginal tax rates, those with higher break-even points, higher benefit guarantees or subsidy levels, and lower marginal tax rates obviously were more adequate in terms of the benefits they would provide and their potential for reducing poverty; they also were more costly. Projected costs of the different proposals ranged from a low of $2 billion annually based on the value of the dollar in 1963 to a high of $38 billion annually. Some costs would have been offset by monies not spent on other income maintenance programs. For example, Milton Friedman (1962), who originated the idea of the negative income tax, would have paid for negative income tax benefits by eliminating what he said was a "rag bag" of measures that included social security, Medicare, public housing, public health programs, farm price supports, and the minimum wage. His goal, unlike President Johnson's, was not to reduce or eliminate poverty, but only to alleviate it to allow the free market to operate to the fullest extent possible (Vadakin, 1968a). Other proponents of the negative income tax were Robert Lampman, James Tobin, Edward Schwartz, and Robert Theobald, each of whom had different goals and objectives they were trying to achieve: Lampman, to provide help to the very poorest of the poor; Tobin, to promote work incentives; Theobald to provide income security to all workers in a world of work displacement; and Schwartz, to eliminate the means test and reduce poverty.

NEGATIVE INCOME TAX PROPOSALS: ASSESSED CONSEQUENCES

True to the rational choice model, all of the NIT alternative proposals were evaluated for their assessed consequences relative to the goals/values they would maximize. The same values criteria that were used to evaluate the consequences of AFDC were applied to evaluating the NIT proposals. As it turned out, all of the NIT plans would have improved the economic situation of families in low benefit states, and also that of families who were not receiving AFDC because of its stigma, although they were eligible to do so. However, for families in high benefit states it was a different matter in that their economic situation would worsen under plans with lower minimum income guarantees and break-even points, plans that were more adequate being too costly to consider seriously. With respect to equity and individual rights, because all of the plans were designed to be universal, applying to everyone sharing a similar income status regardless of residence or family status, they all would have advanced the criteria of equity and individual rights. Further, because none would have required fathers to be absent from the home, they all would have contributed to family well-being (Vadakin, 1968a).

Assessments as to their economic and administrative efficiency were mixed. One of the more attractive features of the NIT when it was first proposed was the elimination of the means test and the stigma with which it was associated. As it turned out, in order to prevent serious inequities and income leakages to the nonpoor, NIT would have required income information that existing tax laws did not, which meant that the means test would not have been elimininated, but expanded, resulting in a universal means test. While its universal application and administration by the Internal Revenue Service instead of the public welfare department (Vadakin, 1968b) might have made the means test more acceptable psychologically, its universal application would have reduced the administrative and economic efficiency of the NIT. Further, in order to determine the subsidy or negative tax payments, income reports would have had to have been filed on a regular basis, their frequency depending on the frequency of the payments. If payments were to be made monthly, the administrative efficiency of the NIT would suffer, but if payments were made annually, the economic well-being of families would suffer. The erratic nature of employment among poor families was an additional potential administrative complication, because of the problems it would have created for calculating the subsidy. Also, for those persons for whom the completion of the necessary tax forms were potentially problematic, the plans promised to be anything but administratively simple.

Assessments with regard to the work incentive effects of NIT also were mixed, although the idea that people would prefer leisure to a higher standard of living and would work only to keep from starving had little support. In this regard, Vadakin (1968a) called attention to the increasing number of dual wage-earner families and the widespread desire for overtime employment, noting that almost 60% of the country's increased productive capacities was taken in the form of more goods and services and only 40% in increased leisure over previous decades. While he concluded that a negative income tax was unlikely to interfere with incentives to work among people strongly oriented or neutral about work, in more marginal situations that involved poorly paid workers performing unpleasant jobs that no one else wanted to do, he thought it could (Vadakin, 1968b). Theobald, of course, was not concerned with incentives, considering the issue moot, since he did not think jobs would be available for most people anyway. And Schwartz also considered the issue moot since he perceived the value of work to be so strongly ingrained in most people that they always would prefer to work than not to work.

Uncertainties about NIT's work incentive effects had implications for its political feasibility. Despite general support for "doing something" to help those in greatest need, public opinion polls showed little support for the idea of a negative income tax (Krislov, 1968), most of the opposition and ambivalence centering on notions of work and income derived through work effort.

Alternatives to AFDC: Children's Allowances

Children's allowances were proposed as another alternative to AFDC during this same period, the United States being the only major English-speaking country in the world that did and does not provide some sort of cash allowance for children. Like the negative income tax plans, discussion of children's allowances also emerged out of the perception that the problem of poverty in the United States could be solved. Arguments for children's allowances were based on three interrelated propositions: one, there was no positive relationship between family need, size, and income; two, because of this, children, especially those in large families, suffered; and three, children represented a substantial percentage of those living in poverty (Vadakin, 1968b). Therefore, proponents argued, priority should be given to alleviating poverty for families with dependent children, both as an investment in the country's future and as compensation for the costs entailed in child rearing for parents (Burns, 1968).

Basically children's allowances are cash payments made to families with dependent children by either employers or government. In all countries in which they are provided all families are eligible to receive child allowance grants as a right, regardless of their employment or income status. For this reason, children's allowances preclude the need for a means test and worry about work incentives. Usually, the allowances are payable until a child reaches a specified age, such as 16, or above that age if attending school (Burns, 1968). In many countries, children's allowances are financed out of general revenues and vary with the age of the child and family size, some countries providing a larger increment to the oldest or first-born child in the family, with decreasing increments for succeeding children. In some countries, the allowances substitute for income tax deductions, while in other countries they count as taxable income; in some they do both. All family allowance plans share a concern about childhood poverty.

In the United States, the allowances were proposed as part of an overall strategy of income maintenance reform that included a federalized noncategorical public assistance program and the expansion and improvement of existing benefit and employment programs to address the income needs of adult populations. This was similar to the strategy that then Secretary of Health, Education and Welfare Wilbur Cohen proposed, except that his recommendations, which did not include children's allowances, also called for national health insurance. Thus, unlike most of the negative income tax plans, the children's allowances were viewed as a supplement to—not a substitute for—existing programs, although because of the allowances, the need for income assistance through AFDC would have been reduced substantially, thus offsetting the costs of the allowances.

The most generous allowance that was proposed in this country was $50 per month per child (Brazer, 1968). It was projected that such an allowance would take three-fourths of the children then in poverty out of poverty, thus directly benefiting the largest single group of the poor in 1968, 23.3 million children and adults living in families with children under 18 (Schorr, 1966). In 1965, 70% of these families were headed by men, almost all of whom were fully or partly employed in low-paying jobs. To offset costs and to concentrate benefits on the poor and near poor, it was proposed that the allowance count as taxable income and substitute for tax exemptions allowed for dependent children. This would have increased the after tax income of very low-income families for whom tax exemptions were of little consequence, while reducing it for higher-income families. The net cost of a $50 per month allowance per child that counted as taxable income was $12 billion. Proposed as a universal rights program for families with dependent children, it also would have been administered through the Internal Revenue Service.

CHILDREN'S ALLOWANCES
PROPOSALS: ASSESSED CONSEQUENCES

Assessments of the consequences of children's allowances for furthering desired policy goals were mixed, centering on issues of efficiency and equity. On the one hand, because children's allowances would have been based on presumptive, not demonstrated, need, automatic with the birth of a child, they would have eliminated the need for the means test and its associated stigma. This not only would have been good for human dignity but for the efficiency of administering the allowances as well, although this might have been compromised because of the need for periodic verification of the continued presence of children in the home to assure that monies were not being fraudulently claimed or distributed. The problem was not with the administrative efficiency of the allowances, however, but with their economic efficiency as an antipoverty strategy in that they would have gone to the nonpoor as well as the poor. For this very same reason, because they would have gone to the nonpoor as well as the poor, their potential political appeal was broad, and strategically they were viewed as a means for fostering social cohesion and integration, reducing the hostilities and bridging the social and psychological distance that separated income groups.

With regard to equity, in that the allowances applied to all families with dependent children, and in addition would have covered families who because of the stigma did not claim income assistance although eligible to receive it, they would have treated all families with children the same—which is what equity connotes. Disregarding the overall strategy within which children's allowances were being proposed, which addressed the income needs of low-income adults, critics charged that the allowances did not promote equity in that they did not include adult populations without children, and in this regard, represented a scheme to redistribute income from individuals and couples without children to those with children, which they regarded as unfair. Proponents argued that children's allowances, unlike the NIT, which would have eliminated many programs, were in keeping with American preference for incrementalism, extending a principle already recognized and incorporated in the income tax structure in the form of tax deductions and exemptions for children; less potentially disruptive to the structure of ongoing programs; and less likely to jeopardize the economic well-being of the recipients of these programs.

Because the allowances would have been payable to all families with children without regard to income, their work incentive effects were expected to be neutral. Many in fact thought that because families for the first time would have enough money to meet basic needs, the program actually would encourage work behaviors. Also because fathers would not have been required to be absent from the home, they would help to stabilize family life, addressing the criterion of family well-being. Questions about the fertility effects of children's allowances were answered by referring to the experiences of countries in which the allowances were a well-established part of family policy. These showed that although the allowances had been established to stimulate population growth, they in fact had not done so. Just as the cost of the negative income tax plans varied with their adequacy, the cost of childrens' allowances plans varied similarly: The more adequate the plan in terms of their antipoverty effectiveness, the more prohibitive were their costs. All of the NIT and children's allowances plans were merely proposals for welfare reform up to this point, all developed by opinion elites, and had not yet taken the form of a bill that legislators could debate on the floor of Congress.

Nixon's Alternative to Welfare: The Family Assistance Plan (FAP)

The NIT took legislative shape in 1969 when President Nixon proposed that "the demeaning and bankrupt welfare system" be replaced with a "new family assistance system" in a message to Congress (The New York Times, 1969). In brief, the Nixon welfare reform proposal, otherwise known as the Family Assistance Program, or FAP, called for a minimum federally guaranteed income of $1600 for families of four up to a break-even point of $3920 a year where "a family head was willing and able to work." The marginal tax rate was 50% on earnings after the first $60 of monthly wages. Individual states could have supplemented the subsidy so that no family would have been worse off with the plan than without it. Every family, including those with fathers, would have been eligible for the program. In an attempt to win conservative support for his proposal, Nixon introduced an "obligation to work" provision into the bill that would have required all recipients except mothers of preschool children to register for job training and work. According to Michael Harrington (1984: 33), Nixon in justifying this maneuver said, "I don't give a damn about the work requirement. This is the price of getting the $1600," the minimum income guarantee which conservative Southern congressional leaders complained was too generous. Thus FAP's work requirement was the bargaining chip for Southern support of the $1600 income guarantee, illustrative of choice under conditions of no or limited authority, as in game theory.

The proposal also called for the provision of child care as a part of the package; the establishment of federal standards for the adult categorical public assistance programs OAA, AB, and AD; the elimination of residency requirements for the adult public assistance programs; the separation of the provision of social services from income; and financially beneficial arrangements to states for administering the adult assistance programs (U.S. House of Representatives, 1970). The estimated cost of FAP was $4 billion annually, but many believed that if adequate day care were provided, its costs would have been considerably higher (Bell, 1970). As it turned out, groups such as the National Welfare Rights Organization (NWRO) under the leadership of Executive Director George Wiley mounted a successful campaign in conjunction with other groups in opposition to FAP whose benefits they regarded as inadequate, whose work requirements they regarded as coercive, and whose day-care provisions, which would have separated FAP children from other children, they regarded as socially divisive and stigmatizing. Further, FAP administratively was enormously complex, and its strong work requirements, which garnered conservative support, became a target of opposition that NWRO mobilized, illustrative of policy as the equilibrium reached in the struggle between contending interest groups.

Other legislative proposals offered during this period to reform the welfare system, in part in response to the criticisms of FAP, included those of the President's Commission on Income Maintenance Reform, known as the Heineman Commission, and of Senator Fred Harris. These also were based on negative income tax principles but varied with respect to their minimum benefit guarantees, their break-even points, their marginal tax rates, and their emphasis on work. Senator Harris's plan included a work requirement for mothers with school aged children; the Heineman Commission's plan did not. The estimated cost of the Commission's plan was $6 billion; the Harris plan, $20 billion. In the meantime the budget surplus that instigated the search for alternatives to welfare had evaporated in the Vietnam war (Harrington, 1984).

McGovern's Universal Demogrant and National Income Insurance Proposal

No consensus yet having been reached with regard to welfare reform, Senator George McGovern in 1972 proposed that every man, woman, and child in the country receive a taxable grant of $1000, otherwise known as universal demogrant (Lewis, 1972a), in replacement of the nation's welfare system. His proposal also called for a change in minimum tax rates and the creation of a system of tax credits to raise the incomes of everyone at the lower end of the economic spectrum to a point above the poverty line; the elimination of preferential tax treatment of capital gains and inherited property; the elimination of the oil depletion allowance; the end of tax write-offs that McGovern said encouraged an overinvestment in commercial buildings, shopping centers, and luxury apartments; and the reduction of the individual tax rate from 70% to 48% for the highest-income taxpayers, the same as for corporations. Such changes, in addition to a $32 billion cut in defense spending, he said, would provide sufficient revenues to cover the costs of his program. For everyone with annual incomes above $22,000 taxes would increase, but decrease for those with incomes below that amount.

Not surprisingly, McGovern's proposal was assailed by Democrats and Republicans alike. Republicans said it would create a huge $126 billion deficit in the federal budget within two years, and according to Herbert Stein, President Nixon's economic adviser, would require an "enormous" tax increase to finance, the proposal to cut defense spending being "an illusory source of revenue because no responsible president would do it" (Lewis, 1972b). According to Joseph Pechman, also an economist, who in coming to McGovern's defense said that an estimated $22 billion in new revenues could be raised just by closing tax loopholes—without raising taxes on income derived from wages and salary. Walter Heller and Charles Schultze, also economists, joined Pechman in acclaiming McGovern, saying that no other presidential candidate had gone so far to promote progressive taxation. At the same time, questions were raised as to how the plan could be financed without creating serious inequities in the tax structure and would mesh with existing benefit programs such as unemployment compensation and social security. Also, despite McGovern's goal to raise everyone above poverty, estimates were that as many as 12 million people still would have incomes below the poverty line. McGovern also was advised of the problems he was likely to encounter as a potential presidential candidate for the Democratic party in countering opposition that promised to characterize his program as a $1000 giveaway, a position made more difficult by the opposition of Hubert Humphrey, his competitor for the Democratic party's presidential nomination.

Subsequently McGovern modified his strategy by saying that he would end the present welfare "mess" by instituting a National Income Insurance Plan, making jobs the cornerstone of his policy. Asserting that the "best answer to welfare is work," he proposed a program of public service jobs estimated to cost about $6 billion; and the expansion of social security to provide minimum payments of $150 per month and coverage to large numbers of aged, blind, disabled, and orphaned Americans who "otherwise would be on welfare," at an estimated cost of about $3 billion. By guaranteeing job opportunities and expanding social security, McGovern estimated that the welfare rolls would be cut by 30% in just three years. For those who could not work or qualify for social security, he proposed a combination of food stamps and cash supplements. Thus a family of four with no other income source would receive $4000 a year in stamps and cash, which, it was calculated, still would not bring poor families whose earnings were below the poverty line over it. Neither McGovern nor Humphrey became president, although McGovern did win the Democratic party's presidential nomination that year.

Subsequent Incremental Actions: Supplemental Security Income, the Earned Income Tax Credit, and Title XX

Although consensus could not be achieved on FAP, or on any of the other welfare reform proposals cited above, legislation was enacted in 1972 that combined the adult public assistance programs, OAA, AD, and AB, into a single federal program known as Supplementary Security Income (SSI), thus achieving some of FAP's objectives. Such incremental action was possible because the populations these programs served raised few issues with respect to work and work incentives. At the same time, regardless of how positive this action was, it created serious inequities between the families served by AFDC, which was and is the only remaining federal-state-county income maintenance program, and the individuals served by SSI, a federal income maintenance program that provides uniform federal benefits that individual states can supplement.

Other actions flowing from the Congressional debates about FAP were the Title XX Social Services Act, a block grant to states for the provision of social services, separating the provision of services from the provision of income, and the Earned Income Tax Credit (EITC) (Garfinkle, 1983), a negative income tax for families with low earnings. Administered by the Internal Revenue Service within the personal income tax framework, the EITC is an earnings subsidy for low-income workers.

Carter's Alternative to Welfare: Program for Better Jobs and Income

No real welfare reform having yet taken place with respect to AFDC, President Carter subsequently proposed a Program for Better Jobs and Income when he came to office. It consisted of two parts: a jobs component and a cash assistance component (Washington Social Legislation Bulletin, 1977). Those in need of assistance were divided into those considered able and not able to work outside the home, or were unavailable for jobs outside the home because of the absence of available day care. Recipients who secured unsubsidized employment in either the private or public sectors would have been rewarded with higher assistance payments or higher earned income tax credits as work incentives. The cash assistance component of the proposal would have replaced AFDC, SSI, and food stamps, creating a single uniform federal cash assistance program based on family size to serve an upper and lower tier of recipients. The upper tier would have consisted of individuals and parents not expected to work: the aged, blind, or disabled, single-parent families with young children for whom day care and jobs were not available, and two-parent families with young children in which a parent was disabled or incapacitated. The lower tier would have consisted of single- and two-parent families and childless couples who would be expected to work. The plan called for a job to replace or supplement cash assistance for those able and expected to work and an increase in tax credits for low wage earners with children. Thus Carter's proposal would have retained the work requirement and incentives of FAP, although in a later revision these provisions were relaxed if no jobs were available in the community in which the person lived. The work program, Comprehensive Employment and Training Act (CETA), stipulated that wages had to be at least minimum wage.

The Congressional Budget Office estimated that Carter's total welfare reform package would cost at least an additional $18 billion over expenditures for fiscal year 1983; some estimates were as high as $22 billion. Like other proposals to reform the welfare system, Carter's proposal for a Better Jobs and Income Program failed to be enacted because it was too expensive, and also administratively complex. Further, it involved a number of structural and institutional issues that could not easily be resolved: a larger role for the federal government in its mandate of federal minimum benefit levels and a plan so comprehensive that it was at odds with the committee structure of Congress, potentially bringing it under the jurisdiction of three committees in the House alone (Wickenden, 1978).

Findings from the Income Maintenance Experiments

In the meantime, research findings from the Seattle-Denver negative income tax experiments involving different levels of minimum income guarantees served to dampen enthusiasm for continuing the search for an alternative to AFDC. The findings seemed to suggest that families receiving an income guarantee did in fact reduce their work effort and dissolve their marriages at a higher rate than those that did not. More specifically, the findings showed that working wives and young people 15 to 21 years of age reduced their work effort 22% and 20%, respectively, and that whites had a marital dissolution rate of 63% at an income guarantee at 90% of the poverty level and blacks a dissolution rate of 73% at 125% of the poverty level (Blank, 1979). Little attention was given to findings showing that reductions in work effort were accompanied by increased time and attention devoted to child rearing and the pursuit of additional education (Robins et al., 1980). Also, at 140% of the poverty level, the marital dissolution rate was only 15% for blacks and 18% for whites (Stanford Research International, 1978), which suggests that at higher benefit levels, the guarantees had a stabilizing effect on family life, an interpretation consistent with the known relationship between family instability and low income from other studies. Had a family perspective been taken in interpreting these findings, more positive conclusions might have been drawn as to the effects of the income guarantee experiments on family life and work behaviors, with a different set of expectations established at the outset.

Findings from the other income maintenance experiments in Gary, Indiana, and the rural North Carolina projects showed other positive family-related findings: families receiving payments reduced their use of social services, thereby freeing resources for other uses; there was a positive correlation between income assistance and health in comparing the birthweight of babies born to mothers in the control and experimental groups; families receiving income support were more likely to purchase their own homes and move out of public housing; and there was an improvement in the school behaviors and scores of children in the experimental groups (Blank, 1979).

Proposals to Reform the Welfare System in the 1980s

Except for cutting benefits and restricting eligibility, the problem of welfare was largely ignored in the early 1980s. Then it surfaced once again when President Reagan deplored "misguided welfare programs" for leading to a "national tragedy involving family breakdown, teenage illegitimacy and worsening poverty (Weinraub, 1986). Contributing to the decision to make welfare a dominant domestic issue in 1986-1987 were the administration's priorities, which centered on reducing the size of the federal government, increasing the size of the military budget, and effecting major changes in the tax law. Subsequently, the Reagan Administration proposed limiting the total value of assistance that low-income people could receive from all federal benefit programs to roughly poverty level, $10,990 for a family of four in 1987 (Pear, 1986), which meant that people receiving assistance would have to choose and manage benefits to meet their specific needs.

In the meantime, the National Governor's Association endorsed a plan that it proclaimed would be the first extensive overhaul of the nation's welfare system in many years, if successful (Herbers, 1987a). Under the governors' plan, all able-bodied recipients, except those with children under the age of two, would be required to find work or enroll in education classes or job training, similar to the Nixon and Carter welfare reform proposals. In return, they would receive medical insurance, day care and other benefits, and the government would assist them in finding jobs. President Reagan in indicating his support for the governors' plan, stated that he intended to submit legislation that called for demonstration projects to test the governors' recommended changes, thus stalling their implementation on a broad scale. Because states such as Massachusetts already had conducted such tests during these intervening years, the governors argued against further test programs. Senator Moynihan as chair of the Social Security Subcommittee of the Senate Finance Committee argued that it was too late to reform AFDC as the nation's main welfare program (Dowd, 1987). The system, he said, had been made obsolete by two "cataclysmic" social changes, the rising number of female-headed families and the rising number of women entering the work force. "Unless we move beyond welfare," he said, "we can assume that some one third of all children being born today will be on AFDC before reaching maturity." He proposed a "new" system that put "its first emphasis on earned income and which, without giving up on the problems of deeply dependent families, extended coverage to all needful ones. . . ," noting that the poverty rate among young children was seven times greater than that of the elderly "a half century after the enactment of Social Security."

The Senator recommended four principles as guides for the replacement of AFDC: (1) parents were responsible for supporting their children; (2) able bodied mothers were responsible for supporting their children by working, at least part-time; (3) the federal government was responsible for providing training, child care, and other transitional services to assist mothers; and (4) that to the extent parent support payments and earnings were inadequate, the federal government was responsible for providing time-limited child support supplements that would gradually decrease as parent earnings increased. As a condition for continued government income support in the event a parent did not secure a job after a reasonable period of time, she would be required to accept job placement in the public sector. Although Senator Moynihan did not offer estimates as to the cost of his proposal, he said that sufficient monies already were in the budget to develop a child support program. "Indeed," he said, "we should end up saving money."

In March 1987 Democratic leadership of the House of Representatives introduced legislation similar to the National Governors' Association welfare reform proposal in its emphasis on education, training, and work (Pear, 1987). Without prescribing national minimum welfare benefits, as some liberals advocated, the bill would require every state to pay benefits equal to at least 15% of its median family income, which meant that 18 states would have to increase their welfare payments. The bill also would require states to pay welfare benefits to two-parent families where the primary wage earner was unemployed; to continue Medicaid coverage for low-income families for up to 15 months for those who work their way off the welfare rolls; and to reimburse welfare recipients for day-care expenses. The estimated cost of the bill was $600 to $850 million for fiscal year 1988, but according to staff experts on the House Ways and Means Committee, annual program costs would increase by at least $2 billion in later years. Under the bill, states could require welfare recipients to attend school, accept employment or enroll in job training classes. Those who refused to cooperate could lose their benefits for three months or more. The work requirement would apply to welfare recipients with children over six years of age although states could impose a similar requirement on parents of children three to six years old. According to the Chair of the House Ways and Means Subcommittee on Public Assistance and Unemployment Compensation, the purpose of the bill was to "make work more attractive than welfare," based on a belief that although the bill would "cost a bit of money at first, it would save a substantial amount of money in the long run as it got people off the unemployment and welfare rolls and onto productive payrolls." A Republican representative contended that the Democrats' bill "provides more welfare but not much reform," claiming that it would make people more dependent on government by substantially increasing benefits in some states.

The national consensus that seemed to be emerging among liberals and conservatives, governors, and congressional representatives and the Reagan Administration in the 1980s was a transformation of AFDC into a job training and placement program. Virtually all of the various interests seemed to agree that welfare recipients should be required to work after a period of training and education if jobs could be found for them; that more public money would have to be spent in the short run if any significant number of recipients were to be removed from the rolls, and that all funds spent on the poor should carry an incentive to strengthen the family rather than "tear it apart," as the present system was perceived to do. Despite the fact that there still was no consensus on how much to spend on reforming the welfare system and the institutional problems that prevented welfare from being reformed in the past remained: disagreement about the respective roles of state and federal governments, the complexity and entanglements of congressional committees, political parties, and government bureaucracy itself (Herbers, 1987b), the possibility of success was considered enhanced because of the way the consensus was created—out of fear that the poor would become such a burden that the well-being of the rest of society would be threatened. These fears were reinforced by the rise of teenage pregnancy and drug use, growing numbers of homeless individuals and families, widening concentrations of poor individuals and families in major cities, and increasing welfare rolls in at least half the states that were economically depressed, despite tightened eligibility restrictions on benefits and benefit cuts resulting from the 1981 Omnibus Budget Reconciliation Act to reduce the size of the federal government.

The secretary of labor spoke of similar concerns when he warned that unless drastic changes were made, 25% of the population would be unable to hold the jobs that will become open by the end of this century. For the first time in recent years many conservatives seemed willing to consider spending more money on welfare if costs could be reduced in the long run. Estimates for the added costs of the work component, including child care, medical insurance, and other benefits were about $1 billion per year in addition to the $17 billion already being spent on existing welfare programs by federal, state, and local governments. Richard Nathan, an official in the Nixon Administration and professor of public and international affairs at Princeton, warned Congress not to "get caught in the FAP trap," which, like the present impetus for welfare reform, was widely popular when first introduced and then eventually was killed in the Senate Finance Committee because liberals and conservatives disagreed over program costs. He also warned that some of the job training programs to which the governors' measure was linked also were in need of reform. Adding that state employment services were 15 years behind the times, he noted that consensus was developing for those reforms as well as for reforms of the welfare system itself.

Of particular relevance and interest were the conclusions the General Accounting Office (GAO) reached after reviewing more than 100 welfare studies completed since 1975, studying case files of more than 1200 welfare families in four states and interviewing federal, state, and local officials. In brief, it stated that there was no firm evidence that welfare greatly discouraged people from working, broke up families, or encouraged unmarried women to become pregnant just to receive benefits (Minneapolis Star and Tribune, 1987), somewhat ironic given the widespread belief that it does and the assumptions on which so many of the current welfare reform proposals are based.

Conclusion

This discussion of welfare reform as a case of family policy hardly deals with all of the related policy developments and experiments during these 20-some years relative to child support, work training programs, subsidized jobs, day care, and tax reform in addition to federal eligibility restrictions placed on AFDC. Clearly, the topic requires volumes, not one brief chapter dealing with welfare reform alone, and volumes indeed have been written about it. Nevertheless, the chapter illustrates several points that merit highlighting relative to welfare reform itself and the objectives of the book as they pertain to policy and families. With respect to welfare reform, several observations might be made: the roles of families and government in relation to each other are being redefined around the issues of work and child support; despite references to families throughout, welfare reform discussions have not evidenced special understandings about families in relation to welfare; values pertaining to work, costs, and the role of the federal government are prominent in all alternatives to welfare reform; research findings that are congruent with existing ways of thinking about work and welfare have more credibility than those that are not, as findings from the negative income tax experiments and the GAO research review illustrate so well; over time, the problem of welfare has been redefined, from one of inadequacy of provision in addressing poverty to the failure of mothers of AFDC families to become self-reliant; and finally, the issues pertaining to welfare and welfare reform, such as unemployment, low wages, poverty, social security, tax and budget policy, transportation, day care, education, training, regional differences in living standards, gender, race, discrimination, occupation, income redistribution, sex, family relationships, and, although not discussed in the present chapter, health and mental health, homelessness, hunger, and so forth—are highly interrelated.

With respect to policy itself, the saga of welfare reform is illustrative of all of the following: policy as rational choice, as evidenced by the alternatives to welfare reform that have been generated and assessments of their consequences relative to the achievement of desired value goals and objectives; policy as incremental choice, as evidenced by the enactment of the earned income tax credit for low-income working families, the supplemental security income program for low-income elderly, blind, and disabled, and Title XX social services block grant, and in the identification and framing of problems for remedial action in welfare reform; policy choice as the equilibrium reached in the struggle between interest groups, as evidenced in the stand-off between welfare rights groups and the Southern conservatives in relation to FAP; policy choice as the preferences of elites, as evidenced by the role that academicians and political leaders have played in shaping welfare reform discussions; policy as choice under conditions of no authority, as evidenced in President Nixon's use of the game approach in introducing the work requirement in FAP to win the support of conservatives; and, perhaps, as evidenced in Senator Moynihan's proposal as well.

Although families' interests in welfare reform are affected, such interests have not always been represented in welfare reform discussions. With this in mind, the following observations might be made, drawing from the family frameworks discussed in the previous two chapters. With respect to work incentives for mothers from the vantage point of exchange theory, recent welfare reform proposals seem to be better informed as to the high costs of paid employment for low-income mothers that come in the form of out-of-pocket expenses for day care and transportation and forgone health insurance, and how these impinge on mothers' work choices. Those proposals that seek to exercise power and coercion to obtain recipient compliance with work requirements, in the manner of conflict theory, compromise exchange theory principles. They also highlight the subordinate and vulnerable position of AFDC mothers as women and as a socioeconomic class relative to male elites who hold positions of government power and make the rules. Efforts to address the stigma associated with welfare could be viewed from the vantage point of symbolic interaction, defining the meaning of the means test experience for mothers, while emphasis on equity could be viewed in terms of relative deprivation, or comparative disadvantage from exchange theory. Each of the proposals also could be assessed from the vantage point of family stress theory in terms of the additional demands they impose on families relative to the resources they provide, and the implications of this for family functioning. Such an assessment might provide clues as to which proposals potentially are the greatest stressors and which the greatest resources, the assumption being that the latter are more likely to attain the policy goal that policymakers are seeking: family self-reliance.

The family perspective that offers the greatest potential in terms of its comprehensiveness, of course, is the systems perspective. It would allow each of the proposals to be assessed in terms of how well they promote family functioning, the performance of family roles, family stability, and adaptation based on the understanding that all systems— families, government, and the economy—are interdependent and interact with each other through their respective input-output processes. Such interactions will be illustrated in the next chapter, which operationalizes them by examining the relationship between state level public policy and individual and family well-being.

References

BELL, W. (1970) "Yardsticks for measuring economic security." AAUW Journal 63: 3.

BLANK, H. (1979) "Senate hearings on Seattle-Denver and other welfare experiments." Washington Social Legislation Bulletin (January 8): 1.

BRAZER, H. (1968) "Tax policy and children's allowances," pp. 140-149 in E. Burns (ed.) Children's Allowances and the Economic Welfare of Children. New York: Citizens Committee for Children of New York.

BURNS, E. (1968) "Childhood poverty and the children's allowances," pp. 3-18 in E. Burns (ed.) Children's Allowances and the Economic Welfare of Children. New York: Citizens Committee for Children of New York.

DOWD, M. (1987) "Moynihan opens major drive to replace welfare program." The New York Times (January 24): 1Y.

FRIEDMAN, M. (1962) Capitalism and Freedom. Chicago, IL: University of Chicago Press.

GARFINKLE, I. (1983) "Income transfer policy in the United States: A review and assessment," pp. 479-498 in E. Seidman (ed.) Handbook of Social Intervention. Newbury Park, CA: Sage.

HARRINGTON, M. (1984) The New American Poverty. New York: Penguin.

HERBERS, J. (1987a) "Governors vote a plan linking welfare to work." New York Times (February 25): 12Y.

HERBERS, J. (1987b) "Consensus on welfare: details later." The New York Times (February 26): 10Y.

KRISLOV, J. (1968) "Four issues in income maintenance for the aged during the 1970s." Social Service Review 42, 3: 335-343.

LEWIS, F. (1972a) "McGovern to give $1000 to every American." Minneapolis Tribune (August 30): 1.

LEWIS, F. (1972b) "McGovern advisers help shape economic, tax policies." Minneapolis Tribune (September 24): 10B.

Minneapolis Star and Tribune (1987) "GAO study challenges welfare theories." (March 21: 14A.

MOYNIHAN, D. P. (1968) "The crisis in welfare." The Public Interest 16: 3-29.

PEAR, R. (1986) "Reagan aides want lid on benefits for the poor." The New York Times (March 2): 1Y.

PEAR, R. (1987) "House democrats offer measure to revise key welfare program." The New York Times (March 20): 1Y.

ROBINS, P. K., R. G. SPIEGELMAN, S. WEINER, and J. G. BELL [eds.] (1980) A Guaranteed Annual Income: Evidence from a Social Experiment. New York: Academic Press.

ROSS, J. B. (1985) "Fifty years of service to children and their families." Social Security Bulletin 48, 10: 5-9.

Social Security Bulletin (1987, December) "AFDC: number of families and recipients by state, October-December 1985." 50, 12: 56, Table M-27.

Stanford Research International (1978, November 15) Testimony before Senate Sub-committee on Public Assistance. (speech)

The New York Times (1969) Text of President Nixon's message to Congress on his legislative program. (October 12): 64L.

U.S. House of Representatives (1970) Committee on Ways and Means. Brief summary of principal provisions of H.R. 16311 The Family Assistance Act of 1970. Washington, DC: Government Printing Office.

VADAKIN, J. C. (1968a) "A critique of the guaranteed annual income." Public Interest 11: 53-66.

VADAKIN, J. C. (1968b) Children, Poverty, and Family Allowances. New York: Basic Books.

Washington Social Legislation Bulletin (1977) "Program for better jobs and income." 25, 17: 55-68.

WEINRAUB, B. (1986) "Reagan assails 'misguided' aid system." The New York Times (February 16): 21Y.

WICKENDEN, E. (1978) "The Carter welfare reform proposal—stage two: From HR 9030 to HR 10950." Washington Social Legislation Bulletin (March 13, 25, 29).

CHAPTER 8

State-Level Public Policy and Individual and Family Well-Being as Measured by State Suicide and Teen Birthrates: A Systems View

The Perspective

This chapter extends the discussion of the previous chapter on welfare and welfare reform to report on findings of research conducted in 1986-1987 on the relationship between state-level public policy choices and individual and family well-being for the 50 states (Zimmerman, forthcoming). The research took a family systems perspective, the family being viewed as a social system in interaction with its environment. State-level public policy was viewed as the output of systemic processes within government structures, such output taking the form of resources that families need to perform their functions; as such they become inputs for families, which families as systems then transform into outputs that in turn become—or potentially become— inputs for policy (Zimmerman, 1976, 1980, 1983). In examining the relationship between state-level public policy and individual and family well-being, the research in effect was examining the relationship between policy inputs and family outputs as outcomes. Terreberry (1972) referred to such processes as the transactional inter- dependencies of interacting social systems. In many respects, the concept of transactional interdependencies is similar in connotation to that of exchange in exchange and choice theories (Ekeh, 1974; Levi-

Strauss, 1969; Nye, 1979), which in addition incorporates the norm of reciprocity as a governing principle of such exchange, which is that people should help, not hurt, one another (Gouldner, 1960). This norm, as will be recalled from the discussion on exchange theory, is considered necessary to the continuation of social life. Essentially it means that everyone's well-being is dependent on social cooperation and the well-being of others (Rawls, 1973).

The Issue

In making the case for welfare reform, President Reagan charged that welfare was linked to family breakup, teen parenthood, and poverty, the implication being that welfare was the culprit that caused these phenomena. Others regarded welfare to be a cause of high state taxes, a perception that led many states to go beyond the budget cuts of the Omnibus Budget Reconciliation Act of 1981 to reduce their welfare budgets even further in the early 1980s. In light of these charges and state-level actions and the discussion of the previous chapter, it seems reasonable to ask: What is the relationship of welfare to individual, family, and social ill-being or malaise? Or to phrase the question more broadly, are there connections between state-level public policy and individual and family well-being, and if so, what are they?

The period selected for the analysis, 1980 to 1982, is important because philosophically it represented a turning point in the history of the United States with respect to the roles of federal and state governments in human affairs. The New Federalism, which gave states increased discretion with respect to the services they provided, for whom and under what conditions, also shifted responsibility for the funding of many health and social service programs from the federal to state governments (Knapp, 1982). Such changes and the federal budget cuts that attended them occurred at a time when the economies of many states, especially those in the Midwest and Northwest were in serious trouble because of foreign competition, high interest and unemployment rates, and technological change. In addition, many states, having passed tax relief measures in the wake of the taxpayers' revolt of the late 1970s, were left with diminished and diminishing financial reserves to fill the fiscal void that federal budget cuts created. It is within this general context that the exploration of the relationship between state-level public policy and individual and family well-being was undertaken. The analysis was based on data from the U.S. Census Bureau and the National Center for Health Statistics.

Definitions

Individual and family well-being were defined in terms of state rates of suicide and teen births, both of which have been identified as serious social problems, and hence relevant to public policy as discussed and defined in an earlier chapter. States vary considerably on these measures, from a low of 7.8 suicides per 100,000 population in New York in 1984 to a high of 27.0 per 100,000 population in Nevada (National Center for Health Statistics, 1986); and from a low of 8.9 births to mothers under 20 per 1000 population in Minnesota in 1982 to a high of 21.9 in Mississippi (U.S. Bureau of the Census, 1986). Although these rates vary from year to year, states in the early 1980s were relatively consistent in their rankings on these measures.

State-level public policy as outputs of governmental structures was defined in terms of states' per capita expenditures for public welfare and education, and state per capita taxes. As defined by the U.S. Bureau of the Census (1985), state per capita expenditures for public welfare include support and assistance to persons in financial and social need, such as cash assistance payments under AFDC and medical assistance; and vendor payments for medical care, burials, and other commodities and services for persons in financial need, including social services. In 1984, states varied in their expenditures for public welfare from a low of $116.27 in Florida to a high of $496.97 in New York (U.S. Bureau of the Census, 1985). A state-by-state ranking of the 50 states on their 1980 per capita expenditures for public welfare, teen birthrates, and 1982 suicide rates appears in Table 8.1.

State per capita expenditures for education include schools, colleges and other educational institutions and programs for adults, veterans, and other special classes; and direct state payments for the operation of local public schools, construction of school buildings, purchase and operation of school buses, and other local school services. In 1984 states varied in their expenditures for education from a low of $228.20 in New Hampshire to a high of $2123.76 in Alaska (U.S. Bureau of the Census, 1985).

TABLE 8.1
Rank Order of 50 States' Per Capita Expenditures for
Public Welfare (1980), Teenage Birthrates (1980),
and Suicide Rates (1982)

State	Teen Birthrate	Suicide Rate	Public Welfare Expenditures
Alabama	46	11	21
Alaska	9	26	46
Arizona	33	47	1
Arkansas	49	23	20
California	23	42	45
Colorado	20	45	18
Connecticut	6	2	38
Delaware	34	30	27
Florida	37	46	2
Georgia	47	33	12
Hawaii	7	7	42
Idaho	18	39	9
Illinois	31	6	39
Indiana	36	15	7
Iowa	15	10	35
Kansas	26	18	26
Kentucky	48	36	29
Louisiana	45	28	24
Maine	27	32	40
Maryland	25	8	30
Massachusetts	2	5	48
Michigan	24	24	47
Minnesota	1	17	43
Mississippi	50	4	25
Missouri	35	21	16
Montana	14	43	17
Nebraska	10	9	8
Nevada	28	50	4
New Hampshire	3	19	33
New Jersey	11	3	37
New Mexico	38	49	10
New York	8	1	50
North Carolina	40	34	15
North Dakota	4	12	19
Ohio	32	22	28
Oklahoma	41	40	32
Oregon	19	41	31
Pennsylvania	22	13	41
Rhode Island	12	14	49

(continued)

TABLE 8.1 Continued

State	Teen Birthrate	Suicide Rate	Public Welfare Expenditures
South Carolina	42	16	6
South Dakota	21	37	23
Tennessee	43	29	13
Texas	39	25	5
Utah	5	31	11
Vermont	17	44	34
Virginia	29	38	22
Washington	16	35	36
West Virginia	44	20	14
Wisconsin	13	27	44
Wyoming	30	48	3

SOURCES: U.S. Bureau of the Census (1983); National Center for Health Statistics (1984); and Book of the States (1982).
NOTE: 1 = lowest; 50 = highest.

State per capita taxes refer to all compulsory contributions exacted by state governments for public purposes, such as sales, individual income, corporation net income, property, death and gift taxes, and motor vehicle license fees. Just as states vary on other dimensions, states vary in their per capita taxes, from a low of $433.43 in New Hampshire to a high of $3946 in Alaska in 1984.

Questions Guiding the Analysis and Discussion

Questions guiding the analysis of the relationship between state-level public policy and individual and family well-being and the following discussion are as follows:

(1) What is the relationship between state per capita expenditures for public welfare and education and state teen birthrates?
(2) What is the relationship between state per capita expenditures for public welfare and state suicide rates?
(3) What other environmental factors account for state suicide rates and teen birthrates?
(4) What environmental factors account for state per capita expenditures for public welfare and education?
(5) What is the structural relationship of the factors that help to explain state suicide and teen birthrates in the study whose findings are being presented?

The following variables and their measures also were examined for their relationship to state suicide and teen birthrates, the study's measures for individual and family well-being, and to state per capita expenditures for public welfare and education and state per capita taxes, the study's measures for state-level public policy:

- Age of population: median age, and age distribution;
- Income level and distribution: median per capita income, income distribution, and poverty rates;
- Gender: male-to-female ratio and percentage of female-headed households;
- Urbanization: percentage living in urban areas and number per square mile;
- Population change: population mobility rates;
- Social integration: divorce rates;
- Racial composition: percentage black, white, Native American, Eskimo, Aleut, Hispanic;
- Education: percentage with 12 and 16 years of education;
- State unemployment rates;
- Individualism, that is, attitudes of self-reliance and independence, minimal government as a preference, cut taxes/cut spending orientation: percentage voting for Ronald Reagan for president in 1980.

Findings

STATE-LEVEL PUBLIC POLICY AND OTHER ENVIRONMENTAL FACTORS THAT IMPINGE ON INDIVIDUAL AND FAMILY WELL-BEING

State Teen Birthrates

The analysis supported the assumption that state-level public policy is important for individual and family well-being. More specifically, the data show that high teen birthrates are related to low per capita expenditures for public welfare, findings consistent with those of Singh's study (1986); they also are related to low per capita expenditures for local schools. Thus, if public welfare really is a factor in teenage birthrates, as President Reagan claimed, its influence is in the *opposite* direction of what he suggested. Indeed, low public welfare expenditures together with high state poverty and school drop out rates, as well as high state unemployment rates account for 80% of the variability in state teenage birthrates. Of these four variables, school dropout rates are the most important, although school dropout rates, state poverty rates, and state per capita public welfare expenditures differ in the strength of their relationship to state teen birthrates by only two to four percentage points.

These findings are consistent with not only those of other studies but also those showing that income transfer programs lift women and children out of poverty at a rate three to five times lower than men (Cassetty and McRoy, 1983). Taken together, they are depictive of states whose opportunity structures are so deficient in the options they offer that low-income and minority teenagers living in states characterized by such structures indeed may perceive early childbearing and accelerated parenthood as their only viable options for achieving the satisfactions they are seeking (Baldwin, 1984). Researchers speculate that in such an environment, females with low self-esteem from deprived and unstable family backgrounds are particularly vulnerable in that they tend to equate sex and sexuality with love, while boys who are more susceptible to peer pressure are encouraged to seek sexual encounters to demonstrate their sexual prowess (Cvetkovich and Grote, 1979, 1980). Low per capita expenditures for public welfare hardly can help matters, since they further deprive already deprived populations of the supports and resources they need to both survive and exit from low or no opportunity structures.

State Suicide Rates

Initial explorations indicated that low per capita public welfare expenditures also are related to high state suicide rates, and quite strongly so. However, other factors, such as high state divorce rates and high state mobility rates have more direct and important effects, and together with a high percentage of persons with annual incomes between $10,000 and $19,999 account for almost three-fourths of the variability in state suicide rates. These findings are consistent with those of other studies based on theories that attribute suicide to economic, demographic, social, and cultural factors (Ahlburg and Schapiro, 1983; Brenner, 1984; Durkheim, 1966; Hollingshead and Redlich, 1958; Lester and Lester, 1971; Maris, 1969, 1981; Stack, 1979, 1980).

As will be recalled, Durkheim developed the construct of social integration to explain societal differences in suicide incidence, that is, as being a function of those characteristics of a society's institutions that serve to bind individuals to the larger collectivity. He held that the rate of suicide varies inversely with the degree of a society's social integration, and that a society having a high incidence of divorce would be considered low on social integration, and thus apt to have more people engaging in suicidal behaviors. Trovato (1986) in noting the historical differences in the relationship between suicide and divorce ascribed these differences to the degree of structural change occurring in society at any given time. This implies that a high degree of structural change accounts for increased rates of family dissolution, and for the individual, severe psychological distress; in Shneidman's terms (1973, 1980, 1985, 1986), heightened perturbation with the sometimes lethal consequence of suicide. The findings of this study certainly would concur with the findings of these earlier studies.

As it turned out, state per capita expenditures for public welfare are indirectly, not directly, related to state suicide rates—in a negative direction—through its direct inverse links to each of the three factors to which suicide is indirectly linked. In that a high degree of structural change is thought to account for high rates of family dissolution, and hence for the absence of social integration, such change also could account for the failure of low expenditure states to address more adequately the needs of vulnerable populations. Higher expenditures for public welfare would connote feelings of connectedness and attachment and empathy with the problems of others and a culture that supports the sharing of cares rather than unbridled self-interest. In this regard, the finding that suicide rates are higher in states that have a large percentage of persons whose annual incomes are between $10,000 and $19,999 has particular meaning given the context of the 1980s. While the incomes of some individuals and families are so unfortunately low that despite recent cutbacks and restrictions they qualify for services and other forms of assistance through public programs, those with annual incomes between $10,000 and $19,999 do not qualify because their incomes are too high—but not high enough to purchase the help they need in the service market, thereby heightening the risk of suicide for vulnerable individuals. That such services can be a mediating influence on suicide rates is supported by Ory and Earp (1980), who found that the use of services among young unmarried mothers was a mediating influence on child maltreatment.

State-Level Public Policy

As the above discussion suggests, variations in public policy among the 50 states in terms of expenditures for public welfare and education are related to variations in state suicide and teen birthrates, both directly and indirectly. Given these relationships and their implications for individual and family well-being, what are some of the factors that account for variations in state-level public policy: state demographics, state fiscal capacity, urbanization, or attitudes toward the role of government and government spending (Dye, 1966; Harlow and Rosen-Traub, 1986; Lammers and Klingman, 1984; Wilensky, 1975)? In the absence of other attitudinal measures, the latter variable was measured by the percentage of states' populations voting for Ronald Reagan in 1980, who campaigned on a cut taxes/cut spending theme, espousing values of minimal government, competition, and self-reliance—in short, a philosophy of individualism.

Findings show that gender, attitudes toward government and government spending, and spending for local schools are the three factors that matter most in terms of state per capita expenditures for public welfare, and together account for three-fifths of the variability in such spending. Of the three, state spending for local schools is the strongest and most positive in influence. This indicates that states that invest more in education spend more for public welfare, the opposite being true in states that invest less. The relationship between the percentage of states' populations that voted for Ronald Reagan in 1980 and state per capita spending for public welfare, not surprisingly, is inverse: States with populations voting in larger numbers for Ronald Reagan spend less for public welfare. Parenthetically, this relationship holds for 1984 as well. The third variable, the percentage of female-headed households in state populations, was positively related to state per capita public welfare expenditures, which also is not too surprising given that such households constitute a constituency that both supports and benefits from such expenditures. This finding is consistent with Preston's (1984) analysis, which highlights the relationship between the growth in the elderly cohort and the increase in social security benefits.

While the positive relationship between the percentage of female-headed households and per capita expenditures for public welfare may appear at odds with the inverse relationship found between the size of the teenage birthrate and state per capita public welfare expenditures, it is important to remember that such expenditures include not only AFDC but Medicaid and other programs that, in addition to AFDC families, are directed at low-income elderly persons, most of whom are women who live in their own households, as well as those who are disabled. Both elderly and younger single women are more likely to maintain their own households because of social security and Supplemental Security Income in the case of elderly women, and, in higher benefit states, because of higher AFDC payments (U.S. General Accounting Office, 1987). Particular attention should be paid to the fact that state fiscal capacity, as measured by state median income, is not an important factor in state spending for public welfare. Thus variations in spending for public welfare cannot be attributed to economics or state fiscal capacity but rather to demographics, namely gender, and to attitudes that govern such spending. What all of this suggests is that states that spend less for public welfare and local schools apparently are unwilling to make the investment needed to address the problem of high teen birthrates adequately, or do not understand the consequences of their failure to do so, in effect perpetuating the very conditions that perpetuate the problem: high state poverty rates and high dropout rates. States that spend less for public welfare also create the conditions for suicide to flourish.

If gender is important relative to expenditures for public welfare, it also is important with respect to spending for education more broadly, not just local schools. In the case of the former, gender refers to a sex ratio that favors males. More males, higher state spending for highways, and higher state per capita taxes account for almost all of the variations in spending for education among the 50 states—90% of it, in fact, state per capita taxes having the strongest influence. What is disquieting about this set of findings is the influence of gender, since what it suggests is that educational opportunities for children vary among the 50 states based in part on states' sex ratio, placing children in states whose sex ratio favors females at great disadvantage. This also has implications for teenage birthrates since states that have higher teen birthrates are states with more females. According to Birdsall and Chester (1987), such demographic data and relationships can be explained by the status of women within a given society or community. Using wage rates and education relative to men as their measures of female status, and taking an economic development approach, they suggest that parents and women themselves tend to invest less in education for women because the return on such an investment is lower for women, given an occupational structure that confines women to low-paying jobs and a wage structure that pays them less than men for the same job. Given that families themselves will invest less in the education of daughters, it seems reasonable to think that states will invest less in them also, particularly when girls themselves choose less costly educational tracks (National Center for Health Statistics, 1984). That sex or gender rather than income emerged as the important influence in relation to state spending for education also suggests that although gender indeed may reflect differences in the income level and distribution of states' populations, it clearly represents more than income level alone.

In terms of state per capita taxes, the revenue source for state expenditure, public welfare and education, the analysis showed that state fiscal capacity, as measured by annual median per capita income, was also not a determinant of state per capita taxes. Nor was spending for public welfare. Nor were state demographics or attitudes toward government and government spending. The only really important factor in determining state per capita taxes is state spending for education, which by itself accounts for almost all—90 percent—of the variation in state per capita taxes. Thus public welfare is not responsible for the taxes states levy, as so often is implied; education is. Further, it appears that states that spend more money for education do so without undue regard for state fiscal capacity, apparently raising the revenues they need to support the spending choices they make, and not the other way around.

STRUCTURAL RELATIONSHIPS OF FACTORS AFFECTING INDIVIDUAL AND FAMILY WELL-BEING

State Teen Birthrates

To better understand their structural relationship, path analysis was undertaken that combined the variables that impinged most on states' policy choices and individual and family well-being. Figure 8.1 depicts a model of the structural relationships of the variables that link to state teen birthrates, which consists of the following:

- states' sex ratio
- mobility rates
- attitudes of individualism
- per capita welfare expenditures
- school completion rates

This model explains almost 80% of the variation in state teenage birthrates, all relationships in the model being statistically significant. The very strong direct inverse relationship of school completion rates

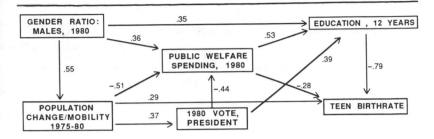

R2 = .79
Adj. R2 = .77
df = 5 ; res. = 44
F ratio = 33.38
Sig. = .000

NOTE: All path relationships are statistically significant at .05 level or lower.

Figure 8.1 Paths to State Teen Birthrates, 1980

to state teen birthrates is important to note. In essence, the model shows four divergent paths to teenage birthrates, two that lead to higher and two that lead to lower rates. One path indicates that states with sex ratios that favor males have higher school completion rates and lower teenage birthrates, and another path indicates that states with a sex ratio favoring males spend more for public welfare, have higher school completion rates and lower teen birthrates—higher state per capita expenditures for public welfare being directly linked to both higher school completion rates and lower teen birthrates.

A third path shows that states with sex ratios that favor males also are characterized by higher rates of mobility, higher levels of individualism as measured by the percentage of the population voting for Ronald Reagan in the 1980 presidential election, and higher school completion rates, as shown by the paths that connect these variables. While these relationships are suggestive of populations that believe in minimal government and are achievement oriented, it should be noted that higher rates of mobility also are directly and indirectly linked to both lower per capita state expenditures for public welfare and higher state teen birthrates. That a higher percentage of persons voting for Ronald Reagan is directly linked to both higher school completion rates and lower public welfare expenditures is worth noting, especially in light of the latter's link to higher teen birthrates. Thus while teenage birthrates are lower when both school completion rates and public welfare expenditures are higher, teen birthrates are higher when higher

TABLE 8.2
Correlation Matrix of Variables in State Teen Birthrate Model

	Teen Birthrate	Education, 12 yrs.	Public Welfare Expenditures	Vote, 1980	Population Change	Male: Female Ratio
Teen birthrate	1.00	−.77	−.49	−.11	.14	−.39
Education, 12 yrs.	−.77	1.00	.17	.35	.32	.58
Public welfare expenditures	−.49	.17	1.00	−.54	−.52	−.10
Vote, 1980	−.11	.35	−.54	1.00	.48	.41
Population change	.14	.32	−.52	.48	1.00	.55
Male: female ratio	−.29	.58	−.10	.41	.55	1.00

rates of population change and a preference for minimal government exert their influence on per capita expenditures for public welfare to make them lower. A correlation matrix showing the bivariate relationships of the variables in the 1980 teen birthrate model appears in Table 8.2.

Except for the sex ratio, these same structural relationships pertain to state per capita expenditures for local schools; however, the influence of attitudes toward government and government spending, while still negative in direction, is less strong than is the case in relation to spending for public welfare. This is not surprising, given the meaning of education for achievement and upward mobility, consistent with the ideology of individualism that underlies such attitudes. These findings are consistent with Wilensky's (1975) analysis, which also notes differences in attitudes toward government spending for education and public welfare in a comparative analysis of public expenditures in 22 of the world's industrialized nations. Nonetheless, although the influence of attitudes of individualism is less strong in the case of spending for local schools, its influence as well as the influence of high rates of population mobility are still in a negative direction relative to spending for local schools. This translates into lower school completion rates and higher teen birthrates without other influences coming into play. In this regard, although not shown in the above model, it should be noted that attitudes of individualism are directly related to higher state poverty rates and through state poverty rates to both lower school completion rates and higher teen birthrates. With respect to the sex ratio, it is

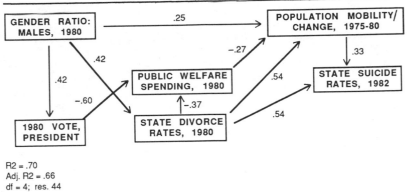

R2 = .70
Adj. R2 = .66
df = 4; res. 44
F ratio = 19.58
Sig. = .000

NOTE: All path relationships are statistically significant at .05 level or lower.

Figure 8.2   Paths to State Suicide Rates, 1982

interesting to note that a sex ratio that favors males is much more strongly and positively linked to state spending for local schools than to spending for public welfare, and through such spending to higher school completion rates and lower teen birthrates. Such gender influence on spending for local schools again raises the issue of differential educational opportunities for children in different states based in part, it seems, on the sex distribution of state populations.

State Suicide Rates

Figure 8.2 depicts a model to explain state suicide rates that also represents a merger of the factors that were found to explain both state suicide rates and state-level public policy as expressed in per capita expenditures for public welfare. It includes the following variables: sex ratio, individualism, that is, attitudes of self-reliance and independence and a preference for minimal government, divorce rates, mobility rates, and per capita expenditures for public welfare.

This model explains 70% of the variability in state suicide rates, all relationships within the model being statistically significant. In this model, the relationship between the 1980 vote and state per capita expenditures for public welfare is much more strongly negative than is the case in the model depicting teen births. As Figure 8.2 shows, spending for public welfare is indirectly inversely related to state suicide

TABLE 8.3
Correlation Matrix for Variables in State Suicide Model

	Suicide Rate	Divorce Rate	Population Change	Public Welfare Expenditures	Vote, 1980	Male:Female Ratio
Suicide rate	1.00	.76	.76	−.45	.39	.40
Divorce rate	.76	1.00	.76	−.42	.39	.46
Population change	.76	.76	1.00	−.52	.48	.55
Public welfare expenditures	−.45	−.42	−.52	1.00	−.54	−.10
Vote, 1980	.39	.39	.48	−.54	1.00	.41
Male:female ratio	.40	.46	.55	−.10	.41	1.00

rates through its combined inverse effects on state population change rates and state divorce rates. It is interesting to note that a sex ratio that favors males is directly and positively related to the 1980 vote without going through population change rates, as is the case in the model depicting teen births. In states in which the sex ratio favors males, divorce rates and population change rates are also higher. In essence, this model points to the potentially lethal consequences of the combination of a sex ratio that favors males and attitudes of individualism as they play themselves out along the paths to suicide. Low on social integration, populations living in states characterized by the variables in this model—a sex ratio that favors males, high rates of divorce and mobility, a population high on individualism and minimal government—appear to be highly vulnerable to suicide, especially in the absence of mediating supports and services that higher per capita public welfare expenditures might provide, attributable in part to attitudes that militate against them. It is important to note that while unbridled individualism may foster individual achievement, its effects apparently can be lethal when combined with high levels of social and personal change and their accompanying losses, and when compounded by the lack of places to turn for help. A correlation matrix showing the bivariate relationship of the variables in the model appears in Table 8.3.

Conclusion

A systems perspective for viewing the family in relation to its environment permits analysis of the linkages between state-level public policy and individual and family well-being. One general proposition flowing from this analysis is that gender and attitudes affect systemic interdependencies and transactions in ways that directly or indirectly lead to higher or lower levels of individual and family well-being. The analysis indicates that individual and family well-being are best served when the transactional interdependencies of interacting systems are governed by reciprocity as a norm rather than the norm of self- or disinterest that underlies individualism. That states vary in their emphasis on which is most important as a guide to public policy is clear. That this has consequences for individual and family well-being also is clear. It is for this reason that the pull-back of the federal government in the area of human affairs is cause for alarm and dismay in that it indicates not only that the norm of reciprocity is *not* the norm in low-spending public welfare states, but that it is *not* the norm at the highest levels of government either.

POSTSCRIPT

This analysis could have taken perspectives other than that of a family systems coupled with the norm of reciprocity from exchange theory. Were it to have taken the perspective of exchange theory, it would have emphasized the costs and rewards of spending choices for public welfare and education, tracing such outcomes through for both families and government, and the larger society as well. Obvious costs would be higher rates of suicide and teen births, or higher rates of poverty, or lower school completion rates, or the disaffection of larger or smaller numbers of people, higher or lower expenditures for public welfare and education, or lower or higher per capita taxes, depending on the value assigned to such outcomes. A conflict perspective would have emphasized the power dimensions apparent in the effects of gender on state-level public policy and the implications of such effects for the status of women and the happiness of men, as reflected in state suicide rates and teenage birthrates, the effects of gender turning on itself, so to speak. Had a family stress theory perspective been taken, the analysis would have emphasized the imbalance between demands and resources that characterize both suicide and teen births as social phenomena, the individual and family disequilibrium and disorganization they reflect, and the role of state-level public policy as a potential resource or stressor relative to the demands of the situation individuals and families are expected to meet. A symbolic interaction approach, which emphasizes the subjective meanings of phenomena, would have been more difficult to use given the nature of the data on which the present analysis was based, although inferences might have been drawn based on what is known from other studies.

The implications of the present analysis for policy itself seem pretty straightforward. Policy based on rational choice would consider alternative strategies and their consequences for requiring both states and the nation to meet higher standards of reciprocity in their transactional exchanges with individuals and families. Policy based on incremental choice would attempt to deal with such issues using past and present experience as a guides, perhaps in developing mechanisms for better intersystem linkages between families and government; policy as the equilibrium reached between competing interest groups would mobilize action to press for greater reciprocity and equality in expenditures for education and public welfare among the 50 states; policy as elite preferences would seek to attain more positions for females as governing elites as a means for making reciprocity the norm that governs intersystem transactions; and policy as the outcome of choice under competitive conditions would seek to calculate the best strategy for achieving greater reciprocity and equality in intersystem exchanges.

In the meantime, the following inverse relationships apply to such exchanges—all directly opposite those implied by the Reagan administration:

> Lower state per capita expenditures for public welfare are related to higher state teen birthrates.
> Lower state per capita expenditures for public welfare are related to higher state poverty rates.
> Lower state per capita expenditures for public welfare are related to higher state divorce rates.
> Lower state per capita expenditures for public welfare are related to higher state suicide rates.

The next chapter is less global in its approach and concerns. It focuses attention on one specific program, the Mental Retardation Family Subsidy Program (MRFSP), for families with a severely mentally and physically retarded child. The MRFSP is a part of the larger policy of deinstitutionalization of dependent populations that began in the 1970s. The family stress framework is used to assess the consequences of the MRFSP for families, illustrating the applicability of another family framework for joining family and policy issues.

References

AHLBURG, D. and M. SCHAPIRO (1983) "Socio-economic ramifications of changing cohort size: an analysis and forecast of U.S. post-war suicide rates by age and sex." Industrial Relations Center, University of Minnesota, Minneapolis. (mimeo)

BALDWIN, W. (1984, May) "Adolescent pregnancy and childbearing: rates, trends and research findings from the Center for Population Research." Washington, DC: NICHD.

BIRDSALL, N. and L. A. CHESTER (1987) "Contraception and the status of women: what is the link?" Family Planning Perspectives 1: 14-23.

BRENNER, H. (1984, June 15) Estimating the Effects of Economic Change on National Health and Social Well-Being: A Study Prepared for the Use of the Subcommittee on Economic Goals and Intergovernmental Policy of the Joint Economic Congress of the United States. Washington, DC: Government Printing Office.

CASSETTY, J. and R. McROY (1983) "Gender, race, and the shrinking welfare dollar." Public Welfare 41: 36-39.

CVETKOVICH, B. and B. GROTE (1980) "Psychosocial development and the social problem of teenage illegitimacy," in C. S. Chilman (ed.) Adolescent Pregnancy and Childbearing. Washington, DC: Government Printing Office.

———(1979) "Psychosocial maturity, ego identity and fertility-related behavior." Presented at the American Psychological Meeting, New York, September.

DURKHEIM, E. (1966) Suicide. New York: Free Press.

DYE, T. (1966) Politics, Economics, and the Public. Chicago, IL: Rand McNally.

EKEH, P. (1974) Social Exchange Theory. Cambridge, MA: Harvard University Press.

GOULDNER, A. (1960) "The norm of reciprocity." American Sociological Review 25: 161-178.

HARLOW, K. S. and M. S. ROSENTRAUB (1986) "State policy-making and political culture: the new federalism, tax revolts, and Texas," pp. 190-203 in M. Gittell (ed.) State Politics and the New Federalism. New York: Longman.

HOLLINGSHEAD, A. B. and F. REDLICH (1958) Social Class and Mental Illness. New York: John Wiley.

KNAPP, E. S. [ed.] (1982) "Trends in state legislation: 1980-81," in Book of the States: 1982-83. Lexington, KY: Council of State Governments.

LAMMERS, W. and D. KLINGMAN (1984) State Policies and the Aging: Sources, Trends, and Options. Lexington, MA: D. C. Heath.

LESTER, D. and G. LESTER (1971) Suicide: The Gamble with Death. Englewood Cliffs, NJ: Prentice-Hall.

LEVI-STRAUSS, C. (1969) The Elementary Structures of Kinship. Boston: Beacon.

MARIS, R. W. (1981) Pathways to Suicide. Baltimore, MD: John Hopkins University Press.

———(1969) Social Forces in Urban Suicide. Homewood, IL: Dorsey.

MOORE, K. A. and M. BURT (1982) Private Crisis, Public Costs: Policy Perspectives on Teenage Childbearing. Washington DC: The Urban Institute.

National Center for Health Statistics (1984, September) S. J. Ventura: Trends in Teenage Childbearing, United States, 1970-81. Vital and Health Statistics. Series 21, No. 41. DHHS Pub. (PHS) 84-1919, Public Health Service. Washington, DC: Government Printing Office.

National Center for Health Statistics (1986, September 26) Final Mortality Statistics, 1984 (advanced report). Monthly Vital Statistics Report 35, 6 (Supp 2) DHHS Pub. (DHS) 86-1120. Hyattsville, MD: Public Health Service.

NYE, I. (1979) "Choice, exchange and the family," in W. Burr et al. (eds.) Contemporary Theories about the Family, vol. 2. New York: Free Press.

ORY, M. and J. L. EARP (1980) "Child maltreatment: an analysis of familial and institutional predictors." Journal of Family Issues 1, 3: 339-356.

PRESTON, S. (1984) "Children and the elderly: divergent paths for America's dependents." Demography 21: 435-457.

RAWLS, J. (1973) Theory of Justice. Cambridge, MA: Harvard University Press.

SHNEIDMAN, E. S. (1986) "A psychological approach to suicide." Presented as Master Lecture, American Psychological Association, Washington, DC, August 24.

———(1985) Definition of Suicide. New York: John Wiley.

———(1980) Voices of Death. New York: Harper & Row.

———(1973) "Suicide," pp. 383-385 in Encyclopedia Britannica. Chicago: William Genton.

SINGH, S. (1986) "Adolescent pregnancy in the United States: an interstate analysis." Family Planning Perspectives 18, 5: 210-220.

STACK, S. (1980) "The effects of marital dissolution on suicide." Journal of Marriage and Family 42, 1: 83-91.

———(1979) "Immigration and suicide." Presented at twelfth annual meeting of the American Association of Suicidology, Denver.

TERREBERRY, S. (1972) "The evolution of organizational environments," pp. 75-90 in K. Azumi and J. Hage (eds.) Organizational Systems. Lexington, MA: D. C. Heath.

TROVATO, F. (1986) "The relationship between marital dissolution and suicide: the Canadian case." Journal of Marriage and Family 48: 341-348.

U.S. Bureau of the Census (1986) State and Metropolitan Data Book, 1986 (Table 1, State Rankings, Households, Vital Statistics, and Health). Washington, DC: Government Printing Office.

———(1985) State Government Finances in 1984. Washington, DC: Government Printing Office.

———(1983) County and City Data Book. Washington, DC: Government Printing Office.

U.S. General Accounting Office (1987, February) Welfare: Issues to Consider in Assessing Proposals for Reform. Washington, DC: Government Printing Office.

WILENSKY, H. (1975) The Welfare State and Inequality. Los Angeles: University of California Press.

ZIMMERMAN, S. L. (forthcoming) "State-level public policy as a predictor of individual and family well-being." Women and Health.

———(1983) "Government and families as interacting systems: outputs, inputs, and outcomes," in E. Seidman (ed.) Handbook of Social Intervention. Newbury Park, CA: Sage.

———(1980) "The family: building block or anachronism." Social Casework 61, 4: 195-204.

———(1976) "The family and its relevance for social policy." Social Casework 57, 9: 547-554.

CHAPTER 9

The Mental Retardation Family Subsidy Program as a Case of Explicit Family Policy: A Family Stress Perspective

The Perspective

That children born with severe mental and physical defects are now able to live long lives, in part because of technological advances in medicine, has implications for families and family policy. The perspective that guides this discussion is family stress within a systems framework (Bubolz and Whiren, 1984; Hill, 1949, 1958; McCubbin and Patterson, 1981; Zimmerman, 1976, 1979, 1980, 1983). The discussion is based on findings of a study conducted in 1982 on the extent to which a Mental Retardation Family Subsidy Program (MRFSP) enables families to care for their mentally handicapped child at home and thus delay or prevent the child's out-of-home placement (Zimmerman, 1984). Because family objectives are explicitly structured into the policy that created the program, it can be regarded as a case of explicit family policy. That the subsidy was viewed as a resource for families though it was provided to meet the special needs of the handicapped child, reflects the perspective that guides this discussion.

Because the situational demands and resources of families vary, it was anticipated that the subsidy's effects would vary accordingly, and that the ratio of a family's demands to resources would affect their plans for the child's long-term care. Such demands might be those that arise during the course of caring for the mentally handicapped child; those that arise during the course of life itself, through normal life transitions that are a part of expected family life events; and those that arise from unexpected non-normative life events that often change lives in minutes, such as a sudden, serious illness or a serious car accident involving a family member, or more happily, a justly deserved coveted prize. Any one or combination of such stressors could increase the psychological, social, and economic demands of the situation for families such that the "stress pile-up" they experience overwhelms their capacity to care for the handicapped child at home, depending on the resources they have for coping with them. Potential resources in addition to the subsidy include family size, age of members, education, income, attitudes, the help of other family members, friends, and community agencies.

The study was undertaken in part out of the concerns that Moroney (1979) also expressed when he said that although all social policies can be presumed to affect families, the nature of their effects was unknown because they had never been systematically examined. It also addressed the specific issue that Castellani (1984) raised concerning the unknown relationship between family support services and out-of-home placement of mentally handicapped children. Using the family stress framework to guide it, the study simultaneously addressed two questions: the specific question of what the effects of the MRFSP are on families with a severely mentally handicapped child, and the larger question of what the relationship is between public policy and families more broadly. The following discussion is similarly guided.

The Issue

Unable to care for themselves, severely mentally retarded children require the ongoing care of their families or community caregivers, and depending on the severity of their impairment, will continue to need such care as long as they live. In 1970 the number of severely mentally handicapped persons was estimated to be about 800,000 (Moroney, 1979). Former practice, based on the belief that it was more therapeutic for them, was to place such persons out of the home in institutions. In recent years this practice has been reversed and now favors preventing or delaying the institutionalization of mentally and/or physically handicapped persons, or returning those who are institutionalized to their own homes or communities, although expenditures still favor out-of-home placement.

In keeping with this overall policy thrust, financial incentives in the form of cash subsidies and tax deductions are now provided to encourage families to care for handicapped members at home, the MRFSP being one such example, and thus prevent or forestall their placement in foster care or an institution. These developments are responses to the spiraling costs of out-of-home placements; to a growing awareness that families do in fact provide important services for members; to a greater appreciation of the extraordinary costs involved in the care of a severely mentally handicapped child, which compete with other family consumption needs; and to a shift in professional opinion that now regards home rather than out-of-home care as more therapeutic for children. The latter is an example of perceptions being shaped by definitions of the situation such that the two are congruent.

The MR Family Subsidy Program

The Mental Retardation Family Subsidy Program as a state-provided resource is a part of these changing definitions and developments. The program is designed for families with a child under age 22 with a primary diagnosis of mental retardation, who is either living at home or in a state institution or licensed community residential facility, and who, because of the subsidy program, can remain in or return to his or her own home. Priority is given to families with a severely multiply handicapped child that are experiencing a high degree of family stress and show the greatest potential for benefiting from the program. Requirements have been liberalized to include families with a child diagnosed as autistic or emotionally or mentally ill, and is functionally but not mentally retarded.

Launched in Minnesota in 1976 with only 50 families, by 1986 the number of families the program served had increased almost fourfold. Initially eligibility for the program terminated with the child's nineteenth birthday, but in 1985, true to the spirit of incrementalism, eligibility was extended to the child's twenty-second birthday, based in part on information reported in this discussion. The maximum subsidy that any family may receive is $250 per month. Based on need more than means, income that a child receives from Supplemental Security Income, a federal-state income assistance program for low-income disabled and elderly people, nonetheless may be taken into account in determining a family's actual subsidy. The subsidy may be used to pay for such items as respite care, special equipment, special clothing, special food, medical and dental care, diagnostic assessments, therapy, and a variety of other family support services (Minnesota Statutes Supplement, 1985) that the child's care entails. Monies set aside by the state for emergencies that require exceptional resources can be used to meet the health, welfare-safety needs of the child for up to 90 days per year.

If the program were to be classified in terms of its social welfare function, using Titmuss's classification scheme as outlined in the first chapter, it would be categorized as serving a compensatory function—compensating families for the extraordinary costs involved in caring for a physically and mentally disabled child. It also represents an income rather than a service strategy for helping families, enabling families to purchase the services they need rather than funding such services directly. In this regard, it relies on a market rather than a political response for the provision of needed services.

The following discussion illustrates the application of the family stress framework, and focuses on the subsidy as a resource for helping families achieve or maintain their demand/resource balance while caring for their mentally handicapped child. Three different sets of questions were used to assess the subsidy's effects on families: the extent to which the subsidy enabled families to care for the handicapped child at home; the extent to which the subsidy enabled families to perform their functions socially, psychologically, and economically; and families' perceptions of the program's overall helpfulness. The discussion is based on the responses of 38 parents who agreed to participate in the study, or 54% of a stratified randomly selected sample of 70 families drawn from the total population of 187 families receiving the subsidy at the time of the survey. This represents a little over 20% of the total population of families in the program. It may be assumed that the 46% of the selected sample who chose not to participate were experiencing higher levels of family stress than those who did. Because of the small number, the usual caveats apply: The discussion should be regarded as illustrative rather than definitive in terms of the effects of one public provision on a small group of families.

Findings

THE FAMILIES

Of the 38 families who participated in the study, almost all were two-parent never-divorced families, somewhat at odds with the general population. In light of the discussion of the previous chapter concerning gender, it is of interest to note that males far outnumbered females, whether the children were or were not mentally handicapped. Number of children per family ranged from one to seven, the average being three. The average age category of mentally handicapped children whose ages ranged from 2 to 17 years was 5 to 9 years. Ages of oldest children ranged from 2 to 4 years to 35 to 39 years, or from preschool to young middle age. Parents' ages ranged from late twenties to 60. Annual family income ranged from $5000 or less to a high of $40,000 to $49,000, average annual income being between $15,000 and $20,000. Fathers' educational attainment level ranged from less than high school to the Ph.D. degree, their average level of education being a little higher than mothers, although fewer fathers than mothers were high school or college graduates with BA degrees. All of the fathers were employed, almost all full-time. A little over one-third of the mothers worked outside the home full- or part-time.

According to parents, the child's handicapping condition severely limited his or her ability to function independently: three-fourths of the children had difficulty toileting by themselves; almost all of the children had difficulty feeding and dressing themselves; over half had difficulty relating to others and in walking. The only areas of functioning not affected by the children's handicapping condition were sight and hearing. Most families had been in the program for less than two years, but four had been in it since its inception; the average wait for getting into the program after application was two to six months. Most learned about the program from their county social service worker, whose professional role is to link individuals and families to needed services, or in systems terms, facilitate intersystem linkages.

THE EFFECTS OF THE MR FAMILY SUBSIDY PROGRAM

Families' perceptions of the overall helpfulness of the Subsidy were unequivocally positive. Indeed, some said that were it not for the subsidy they would not be able to care for their mentally handicapped child at home. With respect to the subsidy's effects on families' capacities to function, the subsidy was especially helpful in enabling mothers to purchase special items for the child; pay for respite care and baby-sitting services; and attend to the child's needs more generally. One mother said that the subsidy also enabled her to attend to the physical needs of her husband, who had high blood pressure and lesions on his kidney and behind his eyes, implying that it freed her from having to make choices between attending to the needs of her husband and those of their child, illustrative of the systemic effects of the subsidy; the "pile-up" of stressors and demands that some families experience; critical competing family consumption needs; and the ethical dilemmas created by such competing needs and demands. Several referred to the financial and psychological security the subsidy afforded them, highlighting the psychological dimensions and importance of the subsidy as an economic resource. One contrasted the freedom and autonomy the subsidy afforded her with the controls and restrictions of AFDC.

The subsidy was less helpful in enabling mothers to keep up with household chores; work outside the home; or engaging in activities at home for their personal enjoyment, activities that compete with the demands of the child's care and the needs of other family members for mothers' time and energy. Most, however, thought they managed better along these latter dimensions after receiving the subsidy than before. And for some, the subsidy was helpful in enabling them to work outside the home. Indeed, based on families' before and after responses to the same set of questions, average family functioning scores were considerably higher after than before receiving the subsidy. Thus the subsidy apparently does enable families to achieve a balance between the resources and demands of their situation and thus care for their child at home while performing other ongoing family functions.

INFLUENCING FACTORS

Factors having a positive influence on the extent to which the subsidy enabled families to care for their handicapped child at home were the ages of oldest children and the length of time families had been in the program. That the effects of the subsidy were more positive the longer families were in the program perhaps can be attributed to both the program's cumulative effects and the transformation of oldest children from making demands into being resources as they grow older. Lending credence to the notion of such transformation was the upper age range of oldest children, young middle age, and mothers' identification of oldest children as helping resources.

Families' socioeconomic status, on the other hand, was inversely related to the enabling effects of the subsidy relative to the child's home care. That is, the higher fathers' educational attainment level and family income, the less enabling the subsidy was perceived with regard to such care; by the same token, the lower fathers' educational attainment level and family income, the more enabling the subsidy was perceived with respect to the home care of the mentally handicapped child. These findings suggest at least three possibilities: one, that the subsidy is less important to families of higher socioeconomic status than to families lower on the status scale either because the cash value of the subsidy they receive is smaller, based on family income, thereby exerting a negative influence on its effects, or that as a function of their higher-income status, the value they place on the subsidy is lower. Another possibility is that because families of higher SES tend to have higher aspirations for their children, which in the case of families with a severely mentally handicapped child can never be realized, the care of such a child may be more stressful for them, thereby affecting the coping effects of the subsidy in a negative direction. In other words, the meaning that they attribute to their child's handicapping condition may be such that it intensifies the stress of their situation, which then acts to influence the subsidy's enabling effects negatively. Not unexpectedly, given its implications for "stress pile-up," the severity of the hand-icapping condition of other children in the family also was inversely related to the subsidy's enabling effects.

Caregiver perceptions of the subsidy's overall helpfulness was inversely related to families' total resources and to the economic environment in which families lived as measured by county per capita income, while caregivers' assessments of the provisions that the subsidy purchased was positively related to their perceptions of the subsidy's overall helpfulness. Family resources took the form of services received from families and friends, from community institutions, and purchased by the subsidy itself. In assessing such services in terms of their availability, accessibility, convenience, quality, and costs, families rated subsidy purchased services higher than the services they received from family and friends and community agencies on all of these dimensions except costs. Thus it is not surprising that ratings of subsidy purchased services had a positive influence on perceptions of the subsidy's helpfulness. Separate from subsidy purchased services, the two community institutions that families identified as being most helpful to them were the public schools and county social service agencies. For most, it was through the latter that they learned about the subsidy program.

The services provided by family and friends were rated higher in terms of quality and costs, but lower on availability, accessibility, and convenience than the services provided by community agencies or purchased through the subsidy. Mothers' primary helping resources were fathers, but older children, regardless of sex, also were important helping resources relative to the handicapped child's care. In those families in which siblings did not assume a caretaking role of any kind, the children generally were younger than the handicapped sibling. It is surprising that maternal and paternal grandmothers, paternal aunts, and maternal uncles were identified as the least helpful resources.

That the subsidy was perceived as being more helpful for families with fewer resources available to help them and to families living in poorer counties that typically offer fewer services is suggestive of the greater significance of the program to families in less advantageous circumstances. In addition, the portability of the subsidy, that is, money, could make families living in poorer communities that offer fewer services less dependent on their immediate environment for the services they need. That the subsidy was perceived as being less helpful in better-off counties perhaps may be attributable to the greater availability of resources in better-off counties, not all of which may require purchase, which then might negatively influence perceptions of the subsidy's helpfulness. Or perhaps it may be attributable to the higher cost of living in better-off counties, which would then have the same negative influence on family perceptions of the helpfulness of the subsidy. Or perhaps the finding was spurious. Castellani (1984) referred to the importance of the environment for family support services in terms of transportation, recreation facilities, and medical, dental and other professional services, noting how much these varied by locale.

Factors having a positive influence on the extent to which the subsidy enabled families to perform their functions along the several dimensions of family functioning discussed above include the age of youngest child, the number of disruptive family life events families experienced in the last six months, and the developmental progress of the mentally handicapped child. Thus the subsidy's effects on family functioning and coping were enhanced as youngest children grew older, just as they were as oldest children grew older, and by the developmental progress of the handicapped child. Most families, although not all, thought their child had improved socially, physically, intellectually, and emotionally over time, despite the fact that most of the children were unable to toilet themselves, feed or dress themselves, walk, or relate to others. That the coping effects of the subsidy also were greater for families who had experienced more disruptive life events just prior to the survey again illuminates the balance the subsidy provided relative to family demands or stressors. For this group of families, such events involved serious economic hardships, such as a sharp decrease in income, the loss of a job, a job change, and the serious illness and/or serious disability of a family member. Such disruptive events also are illustrative of the multiple stressors that families in the study experienced, of which the care of the handicapped child was only one.

FAMILIES' LONG-TERM CARE PLANS FOR CHILD

Despite the very positive effects of the subsidy, half of the families anticipated placing their child out of the home in the future. Families who anticipated out-of-home placement differed significantly from those who did not in terms of family size, employment status of the mother, mothers' age, and the developmental progress of the child. More specifically, mothers anticipating out-of-home placement for their child were younger and had fewer children than those who did not. They also worked outside the home and their mentally handicapped child showed less developmental progress than the children of mothers not anticipating out-of-home placement.

Over one third of the mothers in the study worked outside the home full or part-time, somewhat lower than labor force participation rates and trends for women more generally, but consistent with variations in rates for married women of different ages. Such findings may be due to differences in historical circumstances relative to older and younger mothers' employment outside the home; differences in resources in the form of family size and older children's services, which also could be due to differences in historical and cultural circumstances of younger and older mothers; as well as age discrimination in the labor market affecting employment opportunities of older women, and so forth. Thus it is the case that younger mothers are more likely than older mothers to perform dual family and work roles with fewer resources to help them, and are thus subject to greater stress and demands. This may be a function not only of historical differences in cultural norms governing family size, but also in part of family life cycle stage in that younger mothers have not yet had time to accrue interest and dividends on their childbearing, child-rearing investments in the form of older children's services. Although not identified as primary caretaking resources, older children nonetheless were identified as valuable helping resources.

Current norms for smaller families suggest that the current generation of younger mothers may always be somewhat disadvantaged in this regard.

Discussion and Conclusion

This discussion illustrates the kinds of information that can be obtained from the application of a family framework when examining the effects of a given policy for families. Not meant to supplant other kinds of analyses that are needed for policy development and evaluation, it provides a way for understanding and anticipating certain family behaviors and responses that at first may seem contrary to intended policy outcomes and thus lead to erroneous conclusions regarding program effectiveness. This pertains to the finding that half of the families anticipated out-of-home placement for their child, despite the subsidy's helpfulness. What the framework suggests is that while the subsidy was and is a most important resource in terms of enabling all of the families to meet the demands inherent in caring for their mentally handicapped child at home and thus serves important policy goals by delaying out-of-home placement, other influences are at work that also affect family behaviors and decisions.

The application of a family stress framework also is useful for raising questions about the family subsidy program as an income strategy that relies on market responses for meeting the needs of families with a mentally handicapped child. While such a strategy may enable families to exercise autonomy in the purchase of services that they themselves choose, its effects in creating the kinds of resources in the form of services that families need have yet to be determined. While the findings of the study are suggestive in a positive way, in-depth study from both a family and policy perspective is required to assess the experience.

The application of a family framework also can serve as protection against actions that could threaten the viability of families. For example, that the relationship between family socioeconomic status and the enabling effects of the subsidy was inverse could lead some to advocate for making the subsidy a means rather than needs tested program as a way of stretching and targeting limited resources. A disturbing dilemma for policy choice in a period of fiscal constraint, such a strategy in the case of families with a mentally handicapped child who already are confronted with multiple and competing demands and thus prone to stress pile-up, could be the stressor that upsets the resource/demand balance that the subsidy, as presently designed, seems able to help families achieve. Such a strategy, were it to occur, could threaten not only the viability of families but their capacity to care for their child as well, including that of families not anticipating out-of-home placement, an unfortunate outcome were it to occur, a case of ill-advised family policy. Thus the application of a family framework in looking at the interface between families and policy can yield important insights that can then be used to inform future family policy.

Postcript

The discussion of the Mental Retardation Family Subsidy Program could have been approached from exchange theory in terms of the costs and rewards as outcomes for families with a mentally handicapped child. Indeed, differences in their plans for the child's long-term care would indicate that the costs of caring for their mentally handicapped child at home in terms of time and energy were higher for mothers who worked outside the home and had fewer children than for mothers who did not work outside the home and had more children. For a more complete analysis, however, more would have to be known about the rewards such care brings as well. These could include greater family cohesion and support, as evidenced by almost all of the families in the study being headed by two never divorced parents and the help that siblings provided. If a conflict perspective were taken, the subsidy program could be viewed as part of the overall policy of deinstitutionalization that the state has imposed on families in its attempt to contain the cost of out-of-home placements, often at family, usually women's, expense. If a symbolic interaction approach were taken, mothers' perceptions of the subsidy's helpfulness and coping effects could be viewed as their definition of the situation. Indeed, the mother who contrasted her status as a recipient of the subsidy with her status as a recipient of AFDC is illustrative. A better illustration of the application of symbolic interaction as a framework for understanding the situation of families with a mentally handicapped child is a book titled *Families Against Society* by Rosalyn Darling (1979).

In terms of policy, the Family Subsidy Program reflects all of the policy approaches included in this book: policy as rational choice model, policy as incremental choice, the interest group approach, elite preference, and game theory. In terms of policy as rational choice, the Family Subsidy Program maximizes values of cost effectiveness or efficiency and humaneness (Brandl, 1982), and probably family well-being as well, depending on one's point of view. Policy as incremental choice is reflected in the program's growth and extension to include children until age 22. Policy as the equilibrium reached among contending interest groups probably is reflected in the organizational activity of families with a mentally retarded child that advocate for and against such programs on the child's and their own behalf, as do state hospital staff and other service providers whose livelihoods are directly affected by whatever equilibrium is reached. The initial proposal for the subsidy by a state legislator can be viewed as an example of policy as the preference of governing elites to contain the costs of out-of-home placements. And as a strategy to influence family behaviors to contain such costs, the subsidy program also can be understood in terms of game theory. Whichever policy framework may be used, a family framework also is needed to assess the consequences of policy from a family perspective, one not obviating the need of the other.

The succeeding chapter focuses not on families of disabled children, but on families of disabled elderly members, and not on an income strategy per se, but on a service strategy for enabling families to care for an elderly disabled member at home. Although the issues are similar, they are different in scale and more universal in application, and also involve different kinds of family relationships. As in the present chapter, the family stress framework is used as a guide for analysis and discussion.

References

BRANDL, J. E. (1982) "Toward a fiscal agenda for Minnesota." Corporate Report (June): 40-42.
BUBOLZ, M. M. and A. P. WHIREN (1984) "The family of the mentally handicapped: an ecological model for policy and practice." Family Relations 33, 1: 5-12.
CASTELLANI, P. (1984) "Current options for family support services." Presented at the Human Services Research Institute Conference on Family Support Services, Andover, MA, August 5-7.
DARLING, R. B. (1979) Families Against Society: A Study of Reactions to Children with Birth Defects. Newbury Park, CA: Sage.
HILL, R. (1958) "Generic features of families under stress." Social Casework 9: 139-150.
———(1949) Families Under Stress. New York: Harper.
McCUBBIN, H. and J. PATTERSON (1981) Systematic Assessment of Family Stress, Resources, and Coping: Tools for Research, Education, and Clinical Intervention. University of Minnesota, Family Social Science, Family Stress Project, St. Paul.

Minnesota Statutes Supplement (1985) Section 252.32.

MORONEY, R. (1979) "Allocation of resources for family care," pp. 63-78 in R. Bruininks and G. Krantz, (eds.) Family Care of Developmentally Disabled Members: Conference Proceedings. University of Minnesota, Department of Psychoeducational Studies, St. Paul.

U.S. Bureau of the Census (1985) Statistical Abstract of the United States. Washington, DC: Government Printing Office.

ZIMMERMAN, S. L. (1984) "The mental retardation family subsidy program: its effects on families with a mentally handicapped child." Family Relations 33, 1: 105-118.

———(1983) "Families and government as interacting systems: outputs, inputs, and outcomes," pp. 455-477 in E. Seidman (ed.) Handbook of Social Intervention. Newbury Park, CA: Sage.

———(1980) "The family: building block or anachronism." Social Casework 61, 4: 195-204.

———(1979) "Families of the developmentally disabled: implications for research and the planning and provision of services," pp. 87-96 in R. Bruininks and G. Krantz (eds.) Family Care of Developmentally Disabled Members: Conference Proceedings. University of Minnesota, Department of Psychoeducational Studies, Minneapolis.

———(1976) "The family and its relevance for social policy." Social Casework 57, 9: 547-554.

CHAPTER 10

Containing the Cost of Care for Elderly Disabled Family Members as a Case of Implicit Family Policy: A Family Stress Perspective

The Perspective

Population trends coupled with spiraling costs of out-of-home care have made containing such costs for elderly disabled family members a matter of implicit family policy with implications for family caregiving. The perspective that guides this discussion, as in the previous chapter, is family stress within a systems framework (Hill, 1949, 1958; McCubbin and Patterson, 1981), based on the assumption that the care of an elderly disabled family member is a stressful family situation. That the present discussion takes the same perspective as the previous chapter indicates that the care of an elderly disabled family member and the care of a mentally handicapped child are similar kinds of family situations. While such care is known to involve considerable stress for individual families (Hall, 1980), this can vary depending on other demands families are expected to meet and other resources they have for meeting them. In the previous chapter, the focus was on the effects of a cash subsidy to enable families to purchase the provisions needed to enable them to care for their child at home; in the present chapter, the focus is on the effects of adult day care as a resource families can purchase to help them care for an elderly disabled member at home. Since one of the objectives for creating programs such as adult day care and other community-based services is to delay or prevent placement of elderly persons in nursing homes, the balance families are able to achieve between the demands of their situation and their resources for meeting them can be expected to be a critical factor in furthering this objective. A systems view suggests that although adult day care is aimed at elderly disabled members, it necessarily affects their families as well, particularly those family members who assume responsibility for their care. This discussion is meant to extend the discussion of earlier chapters by illustrating the applicability of the family stress framework to the caregiving situation of families of elderly disabled members who attend adult day care, and the nature of the information it can provide as feedback for policy. Undertaken out of the same concerns that instigated the other studies whose findings have been reported in these discussions, the examination of the coping effects of adult day care for families of severely disabled elderly members extends the question of what the relationship is between public policy and families to yet another group of families and set of policy issues.

The Issue

The fastest growing population in the United States is the cohort 85 years and older. In 1984 it was 21 times larger than in 1900 (American Association for Retired Persons and Administration on Aging, 1985), and by the early decades of the twenty-first century it is estimated to reach 8 million (Rich and Raum, 1984). With advancing age, persons are more likely to experience chronic illness and disability, attended by limitations on their capacity to function such that they are likely to need the care of others in order to do so. Because of the growing population of very old persons and the increased costs of out-of-home care, efforts to contain the escalating costs of care have intensified. Alternatives to nursing home placement are being promoted through the diversion of Medicaid and Medicare funds from nursing home and hospital care to community-based services, such as adult day care. Adult day care is for persons 60 years of age and older who have a mental, physical, or social disability that impairs their functioning and socially isolates them. The primary objectives of most day-care programs are to "provide an alternative to premature or inappropriate institutionalization" and to "maximize functional capacity" (National Institute of Adult Day Care, 1985).

According to the National Institute on Adult Day Care, every state in the country has at least one day-care program; California, Florida, Massachusetts, and Minnesota have 85, 56, 65, and 61, respectively. Nationwide, such programs numbered an estimated 1200 in 1985. They expanded even more rapidly in the 1980s than in the 1970s, and are destined to grow even more in the coming years. Most day-care programs offer a range of health and social services, such as individual and family counseling, remotivation therapy, nursing care, diet and nutrition counseling, transportation to and from programs and occupational therapy in the form of arts and crafts. Many in addition provided information and referral services, reality orientation, behavior modification, health education, recreational therapy, group counseling services, and activities of daily living. Persons may attend day care for as little as one day or as many as five days per week. Average per diem cost is $27. Generally speaking, programs do not accept persons who are incontinent, behaviorally disruptive, wheelchair bound, or in need of constant supervision (National Institute for Adult Day Care, 1985). In 1985, only 15 states required programs to meet state established standards for licensure, but programs are required to meet certain criteria in order to certify for Medicaid and Medicare reimbursement.

Other provisions consistent with cost containment policies promoting alternatives to nursing home care are tax incentives that encourage and recognize the contribution of families to the care of older person. Some states in addition offer alternative care grants to help low-income elderly persons pay for the costs of adult day care and nursing home care alternatives. An underlying assumption of all of these provisions is that they will delay or prevent the nursing home placement of elderly disabled members, and thus contain the costs of out-of-home care. Thus the issues that pertain to the out-of-home placement of mentally handicapped children also pertain to the out-of-home placement of the disabled elderly. However, because the number of persons 85 years and older is growing so rapidly, they are of a different dimension, both qualitatively and quantitatively. Complicating the problem is the changing support ratio—fewer adult children 18-64 years of age relative to elderly parents (National Center for Health Statistics, 1983; U.S. Bureau of the Census, 1983)—which means that a larger population of elderly parents will require more help from a smaller population of adult children in the years to come.

In contrast to the family subsidy program discussed in the previous chapter, adult day care represents a service rather than an income strategy for meeting the needs of elderly members and through them, their families, although both strategies are highly interdependent in terms of achieving desired policy objectives. Illustrative are state alternative care grants and Medicaid as income assistance programs to help low-income disabled elderly persons purchase adult day care and other health-related services. Because many of these measures do not have stated family objectives but nonetheless affect the families of elderly disabled persons, some more directly than others, they are representative of implicit family policy. Within the context of Titmuss's framework of social welfare, adult day care and related measures can be viewed as an increment to individual and family well-being. The questions that this discussion addresses are as follows: To what extent does adult day care enable families to cope with the care of their elderly disabled members, and thus delay or prevent their out-of-home placement? What other family resources or stressors strengthen or weaken day care's effects in this regard?

Previous Work: The Caregiving of Elderly Family Members

Findings from earlier studies provided clues to some of these questions. Spouses, for example, are known to assume the primary caregiving role when spouses become chronically ill or disabled (Treas, 1977), but because women live longer than men—seven years for whites and eight years for blacks (U.S. Bureau of the Census, 1985), wives more frequently are caregivers of husbands than husbands are caregivers of wives: 75% and 40%, respectively (U.S. Bureau of the Census, 1983). When a spouse is not available, the role shifts to adult children, primarily daughters (Shanas, 1979; Sussman, 1976), unmarried daughters providing more help than their married sisters, regardless of the presence or absence of children at home (Stoller, 1983), which could be a critical factor in the success of a long-term care policy that depends on family members for its implementation. That sons provide more help if they have children under six, the age when children begin to attend school all day, suggests that such help probably has more to do with daughters-in-law than sons, whose lives are likely to be less affected by their child's full-day transition into school. For daughters-in-law, however, such a transition could facilitate their own transition into a career or job or educational preparation for either, which then might compete with the time they have for meeting the caregiving needs of elderly parents-in-law.

Attention has tended to focus on the stress that caring for elderly parents creates for younger daughters, especially those who work outside the home and have young children, and thus are required to meet demands from multiple sources. Stoller (1983), however, advises that caring for parent actually could be more stressful for older daughters, many of whom may be entering old age themselves and thus do not have the physical or emotional energy for meeting the caregiving demands of an elderly disabled parent.

Many families draw on community resources to help them in this regard. This varies, however, with the level of the older person's impairment and family structure and socioeconomic status. Giele (1984) found that female-headed families were three to four times more likely to seek help from outside sources than families headed by both a male and female, illustrative of the balance families seek to maintain when faced with demands that exceed their structural capacity to meet them. The use of outside resources also was greater when the elderly member's level of impairment was greater, thereby increasing the demands of the caregiving situation, which also is illustrative of the balance families seek to maintain between demands and resources in caregiving situations. While children of higher socioeconomic status tend to purchase the services their elderly parents need, children of lower socioeconomic status are likely to provide such services directly themselves. Such differences in the provision of services by children for parents may be attributed to differences in financial resources and geographic proximity. Children of higher socioeconomic status tend to be geographically mobile and thus less likely to live in the same community as their parents, making the provision of direct help impractical; further, unlike their brothers and sisters of lower socio-economic status, they have the financial resources to pay for help.

Earlier studies indicate that adult day care as one of the community resources that families can purchase helps to maintain the elderly person's physical functioning as well as the psychological functioning of the family (McCuan-Rathbone, 1975), in keeping with the system's perspective. Counseling services and social activities for families coupled with frequent telephone contacts that staff initiated were found to enhance day care's resource potential for families (Dilworth-Anderson and Hildreth, 1982). Because day care diverted and thus reduced the demands of caring for elderly parents on families, Sanders and Seelbach (1981) concluded that it strengthened the capacity of families to care for their older family member. That the use of programs such as adult day care depends on their availability (Wan and Arling, 1983) and their availability depends on the environment in terms of constituent demand and a market or political response to identified need highlights the importance of the environment relative to caregiving of elderly family members by families. As Eulau and Prewitt (1973) noted, "A unit is not set off from its environment, but is a part of it."

Findings from a telephone survey of a population of 94 caregivers of elderly disabled persons attending three different adult day-care programs in three contiguous counties in a seven-county metropolitan area in Minnesota, 87% of whom participated in the survey (Zimmerman, 1986), are consistent with those of these earlier studies. The following discussion, which is based on these findings, focuses on adult day care as a resource for enabling families to cope with the demands of their situation and thus for preventing or delaying the out-of-home placement of the older person. In that neither the caregivers nor the day-care programs were randomly selected, the discussion refers only to the population of caregivers who actually participated in the survey.

Findings

THE CAREGIVERS AND THEIR FAMILIES

As in other studies, the caregivers and their families who are the focus of this discussion were primarily wives, daughters, and daughters-in-law. Daughters were more likely to be caregivers than mothers, either because mothers were the disabled member or deceased. Other caregivers included the older person's mother, sister, sister-in-law, granddaughter-in-law, and great niece. Their ages ranged from 27 to 82 years; their average age was 54. Most were married and had an average of three children, most of whom no longer lived at home. Number of children per family ranged from none to eight, most of whom were males, one caregiver reporting having as many as seven sons and two as many as six. The average age of oldest child was 29; average age of youngest child was 20. Husbands and daughters were caregivers' primary family-help resources, sons assuming little responsibility in this regard, which also is consistent with other studies. Almost half the caregivers worked outside the home, full- or part-time. Over half had some college education. Average annual family income was between $15,000 and $20,000; six reported having annual incomes over $50,000. Almost all were white, two-thirds being Protestant and one-third Catholic.

Most of the older disabled members lived with their spouse or an adult child, most of whom were daughters, but a small percentage lived alone. Ages of older persons ranged from 47 to 94; their median age was 77. Males and females were about evenly divided, somewhat at odds with the sex distribution for that age group more generally. Three-fourths had been disabled for over 2 years, some for 20 years or longer. The high prevalence of Alzheimer's and Parkinson's disease in this group is reflected in their functional capacities. Seventy percent had difficulty walking; almost three-fifths had difficulty relating to others; almost half had difficulty communicating with others; two-fifths also had difficulty seeing; one-third had difficulty hearing; over one-fifth had difficulty toileting themselves.

The Effects of Adult Day Care
on the Caregiving Situation

As in other studies, adult day care was an important resource for enabling the families to restore or maintain the balance between the resources and demands of their situation. It was most helpful in enabling 50% to 80% of the caregivers to, in order of descending frequency, attend to the older person's needs; attend to their own needs; do household chores; enjoy being with family; do things with family; and make needed purchases. It also was important, in order of descending frequency, in enabling 15% to 49% of the caregivers to be with friends occasionally; engage in recreation outside the home; attend to needs of other family members; work outside the home; and attend church. However, until the demands of the situation were such that family functioning was affected, most caregivers thought they managed well in these areas before the older member was in adult day care also. These demands came in the form of such stressors as the serious disability, illness, or death of a family member; the loss of income, the loss of a job, and a job change, all of which are health and income related.

That adult day care helped families achieve the psychological equilibrium needed to care for the older person at home is illustrated by some caregivers' comments when asked what they liked best about day care, such as, "It gives me freedom from her constantly bugging me—I don't have to be her only friend." Other comments expressed similar sentiments, that by providing an opportunity for the older person to socialize with others away from home, it gave caregivers time to be by themselves and for themselves. As a consequence, their feelings toward the older person were more positive. Such comments as "I like her better as a person—she is more interesting," or "I always used to say, 'I might as well be alone,' but now we talk, he talks to the kids" are illustrative. Indicative of the strain that the care of an older family member can create for family relationships and the instrumental role that day care can play as a buffer in these relationships was the terse comment of one caregiver who when asked what she liked best about day care, said, "It has helped me tolerate her." Further, because caregivers were no longer were as dependent on other family members for helping with the care of the older person, their relationship to other family members also was better. Many commented they were more relaxed, one confiding, "I no longer fly off the handle with them from holding it with her."

INFLUENCES ON COPING EFFECTS OF ADULT DAY CARE

Factors that contributed to 43% of the variability of the coping effects of adult day care were: perceptions of day care's helpfulness in enabling caregivers to care for the older person, the older person's being male; number of sons in the family; the alternative care grant; and perceptions of the helpfulness of counseling. The influence of all of these variables except number of sons was in a positive direction: Caregivers with fewer sons as potential helping resources regarded day care as more helpful in enabling them to care for the older person than caregivers with more sons.

Such variability relative to gender can be better understood if gender is regarded as both a potential resource and a stressor. As noted earlier, most of the caregivers were women: wives, daughters, and daughters-in-law whose ages ranged from 27 to 82 years. Most were married and had an average of three children, most of whom were sons, number of sons per caregiver ranging from one to seven.

That the coping effects of day care were greater for caregivers with fewer sons and when the older person was male suggests that the caregiving of males is more difficult and stressful than the caregiving of females, particularly for those caregivers who have fewer sons as resources. This may be so for a number of reasons: males generally have not been socialized to engage in more restricted home-centered activities, and thus when disabled, may be more demanding of caregivers' time and energies; psychologically, the implications of disability may be more serious for males than for females because of the restrictions it places on their mobility and the dependencies it creates on others; such role changes may be further complicated if the disability occurred simultaneously with the transition into retirement; they also may be complicated by cross-gender, intergenerational relationships involving daughters or daughters-in-law, or in the case of wives, spousal relationships; the physical demands of caring for males in general may be more problematic in that women may not have the physical stamina or strength required for giving such care over the long term; also because males typically tend not to deal with relationship problems, problems not resolved earlier in families' history may be carried into later life, adding to the complexities and stress of an already stressful situation.

That the coping effects of adult day care were strengthened for caregivers who had fewer sons upon whom they could draw upon as resources for help again highlights the interdependent nature of family/community resources and relationships. Indeed, fewer sons might mean less physical as well as financial help for caregivers in that sons tend to contribute financially to the care of elderly parents. This helps to explain the importance of the alternative care grant for helping low-income elderly persons meet day-care costs, which served to strengthen day care's coping effects for families, and also again highlights the importance of community resources as a balance for families' resource deficiencies. Fewer sons also could mean fewer same gender interests to be shared with homebound elderly disabled fathers.

LONG-TERM CARE PLANS FOR OLDER PERSONS

Despite the very positive influence of adult day care in terms of enabling caregivers to cope with their situation and the improvement they reported in the older person's functioning: socially, emotionally, physically, and intellectually, making such comments as "he's more alert," "he talks more," "he doesn't feel so sorry for himself now that he sees others in worse shape," and "he interacts more," half anticipated placing the older person in a long-term care facility in the future. Health reasons were paramount: the older person's failing health, caregivers' health, and the health of other family members. In general, the greater the older person's level of impairment, the more likely nursing home placement was anticipated. Most of the elderly persons, it will be recalled, had difficulty walking and relating to others, almost half had difficulty communicating with others, a high percentage had difficulty seeing and hearing, and over one-fifth had difficulty in toileting themselves. Thus, given the level of the older person's impairment and deteriorating health, it is not surprising that caregivers who perceived the coping effects of day care to be greatest were those most likely to anticipate out-of-home placement.

Married caregivers also were more likely to anticipate such placement as were those who gave lower ratings to families in terms of the help they provided. Again, such influences must be seen within the context of the caregiving situation itself. Most of the elderly disabled persons, as noted earlier, lived with their spouse or adult child whose ages ranged from 27 to 82, while the average age of the disabled persons, half of whom were males, was 77, with ages ranging from 47 to 94 years. Thus, although many of the women caring for a disabled spouse or parent were younger, many were not, which means many were unlikely to have the emotional or physical energies necessary for meeting caregiving demands, the over-time cumulative effects of caregiving itself being a drain on the energies they may have once had. As noted earlier, three-fourths of the elderly persons had been disabled for over 2 years, some for as long as 20.

In light of the nature of the older person's disability and the ages of caregivers, it is not surprising that caregivers who were married and who gave lower ratings to families in terms of the help they provided anticipated out-of-home placement. Being married has demands of its own that compete with the demands of caregiving. Dissatisfactions with the level of help other family members provide compounds the stress. Although services provided by family and friends in general rated high in terms of quality, accessibility, availability, reliability, convenience, and cost, there was considerable variability in these ratings, and in general family-provided services were not rated as highly on these dimensions as the services caregivers received from adult day care. In general, this combination of influences suggests that caregiving situations are rife with conflicting demands and expectations on the part of both caregivers and other family members. Given all of the above, it is not surprising that counseling services was one of the resources that helped to strengthen the coping effects of day care for caregivers.

Summary and Conclusion

Again, the application of the family stress perspective within a systems framework proved useful for providing ways of understanding the demands entailed in the caregiving of an elderly family member. Again, it was able to show that despite alternatives such as adult day care, influences within the family situation itself may be such as to preclude prevention of out-of-home placement. A family stress perspective suggests that although programs such as adult day care clearly can delay out-of-home placement, they cannot forever prevent it for those whose disability and health are such that they overwhelm caregivers' coping capacities. It also suggests that adult day care probably can prevent nursing home placement of those likely to need it least: elderly disabled persons who are female with a low to moderate level of impairment, whose caregivers are not married and are satisfied with the help family and friends provide. While such a conclusion may be at odds with the higher nursing home utilization rates for elderly females in the general population, this is attributable to their longer life expectancy. This suggests that political pressures to contain the costs of out-of-home care eventually must yield to the reality that in general, persons of very advanced age are likely to require nursing home care regardless of the community resources families have available to draw upon to help them. This also highlights the fact that just as disabled members grow older, caregivers do too, and eventually they may need their own caregiver.

This is not to negate the importance of adult day care or other community provisions as resources that enable caregivers to care for the older person at home, helping them to better attend to the person's needs as well as their own, and improving family relationships in the process. Indeed, the findings as interpreted from the vantage point of family stress indicate that community provisions such as adult day care do enable families to care for their older member at home and are resources that help to balance caregiving demands. As such, they are instrumental in at least delaying out-of-home placement, and perhaps preventing it under favorable circumstances. In either case, such provisions serve to advance policy goals that have no stated family objectives, although they do affect families, directly or indirectly, illustrating what is meant by implicit family policy. The interpretations that the family stress framework provides speak to the limits to which such policy goals ought to apply.

Postscript

This discussion, like each of the previous illustrative chapters, could have been approached from any one of the family frameworks presented in this book. Family stress within a systems perspective was selected in this chapter because of previous work suggesting that the caregiving of an elderly disabled member is stressful for families. Other perspectives with respect to the caregiving of an elderly disabled member would have yielded insights different from those gleaned from the perspective that was taken. If the issue had been approached from an exchange perspective, the discussion might have highlighted a situation of high costs and few rewards for families, mitigated perhaps by the value caregivers assigned to their relationship to the older person, based in part on their prior relationship and feelings toward the older person, their religious and cultural background, gender, marital, and socioeconomic status, and so forth. If a conflict perspective had been taken, the discussion would have highlighted the conflicts that families experience concerning the care of the older person, the negotiations that take place around it in the bargaining of time and arrangements, and which members' interests generally prevail and why. If the situation had been approached from the vantage point of symbolic interaction, more emphasis would have been placed on the meanings that caregiving had for families, the history they shared with the older person and each other, and their definition of the situation as it was at that moment. Some of that information was obtained when caregivers commented on what they liked best about adult day care, which gave clues as to the meanings of the situation for them. Any one of these approaches also would have been useful for understanding the influences that were determinants of families' out-of-home placement plans, but in ways different from the understandings achieved from the vantage point of family stress within a systems framework.

Social and health provisions in the community to contain the cost of out-of-home care represent policy as rational choice, policy as incremental choice, policy as the equilibrium reached among contending interest groups, as the preference of ruling elites, and choice in a situation where there is no best choice, as in game theory. In terms of policy as rational choice, such provisions are the alternative to high cost out of home placement. As incremental choice, they represent incremental responses to the pressures of increasing numbers of elderly disabled persons and the pressures of high costs and cost containment.

As the equilibrium reached among contending interest groups, such provisions could represent the outcome of a struggle among a variety of organizations and providers competing for Medicaid and Medicare reimbursement or for garnering prized service contracts from state and county agencies. As the preference of ruling elites, governors, and other public officials often refer to such provisions in terms of their own parents, viewing them as being more respectful of human dignity and cost effective. In this regard, it is ironic to note that in one mad effort to reduce state government spending further, legislators in one state—the governing elites—targeted community-based services for budget cuts, which of course only would have increased the costs of out-of-home care. Finally, such provisions might be viewed in terms of game theory, a situation in which there is no best choice, as indeed seems to be the case, given present demographic data and trends. Again the use of a policy framework for assessing the consequences of a given policy does not preclude the use of a family framework, both being needed to provide understandings in attending to a particular policy situation, issue, or problem. In this regard, a family framework can provide information useful for anticipating problems and creating solutions that may prevent such problems from escalating into larger ones.

This chapter concludes the illustrative applications of family frameworks to situations in which family and policy issues are joined. That these latter two chapters are similar in perspective is indicative of the applicability of the perspective to many different family situations. Different from the chapter on welfare reform as a case of family policy that had no family framework to guide it and from the discussion concerning the systemic relationship between state-level public policy and individual and family well-being—they all represent approaches to understanding family policy and the connections between policy and families. The next and final chapter will summarize the book's discussion, discuss the potential of the concept of family policy, and make some final points with respect to present approaches to family policy.

References

American Association of Retired Persons and the Administration on Aging (1985) A Profile of Older Americans, 1985. Washington, DC: Program Resources Department, U.S. Department of Health and Human Services.

CANTOR, M. H. (1983) "Strain among caregivers: a study of experience in the United States." Gerontologist 23: 507-604.

CICIRELLI, G. (1981) Helping Elderly Parents. Boston: Auburn House.

DILWORTH-ANDERSON, P. and G. J. HILDRETH (1982) "Administrators' perspectives on involving the family in providing day care services for the elderly." Family Relations 31: 343-348.

EULAU, H. and K. PREWITT (1973) Labyrinths of Democracy's Adaptations, Linkages, Representation and Policies in Urban Politics. Indianapolis: Bobbs-Merrill.

GIELE, J. Z. (1984) "A delicate balance: the family's role in the care of the handicapped." Family Relations 33: 213-218.

HALL, E. (1980) "Acting one's age: new rules for old." Psychology Today 13: 56-80.

HILL, R (1958) "Generic features of families under stress." Social Casework 49: 139-150.

———(1949) Families under Stress. New York: Harper.

McCUBBIN, H. I. and J. PATTERSON (1981) Systematic Assessment of Family Stress, Resources and Coping: Tools for Research, Education and Clinical Intervention. University of Minnesota, St. Paul.

McCUAN-RATHBONE, E. (1976) "Geriatric day care: a family perspective." Gerontologist 16: 517-521.

National Center for Health Statistics (1983) B. Feller: Americans Needing Help To Function at Home. Vital and Health Statistics, no. 92. DHHS Pub. (PHS) 83-1250. Hyattsville, MD: Public Health Service.

National Institute for Adult Day Care (1985) Adult Day Care in America. Washington, DC: National Council on Aging. (mimeo)

RICH, B. M. and M. BAUM (1984) "The aging: a guide to public policy." Pittsburgh: University of Pittsburgh Press.

SANDERS, L. T. and W. C. SEELBACH (1981) "Variations in preferred care alternatives of the elderly: family versus nonfamily sources." Family Relations 30, 3: 447-451.

SHANAS, E. (1979) "The family as a social support system in old age." Gerontologist 19: 169-174.

STOLLER, E. P. (1983) "Parental caregiving by adult children." Journal of Marriage and Family 45, 4: 851-858.

SUSSMAN, M. (1976) "The family life of old people," pp. 415-449 in R. Binstock and E. Shanas (Eds.) Handbook of Aging and the Social Sciences. New York: Van Nostrand Rheinhold.

TREAS, J. (1977) "Family support systems for the aged: some social and demo graphic considerations." Gerontologist 17: 486-491.

U.S. Bureau of the Census (1985) Statistical Abstract of the United States. Washington, DC: Government Printing Office.

———(1983) Current Population Reports. Series P 23, no. 128: America in Transition: An Aging Society. Washington, DC: Government Printing Office.

WAN, T. and G. ARLING (1983) "Differential use of health services among disabled elderly." Research on Aging 5, 3: 411-432.

ZIMMERMAN, S. L. (1986) "Adult day care: correlates of its coping effects on families with an elderly disabled member." Family Relations 35, 2: 305-312.

PART IV
THE POTENTIAL OF FAMILY POLICY

CHAPTER 11

The Case for Understanding Family Policy: A Summing Up

Although this chapter concludes the book's discussion, it does not mean that other illustrations of the connections between families and policy could not be presented, but only that the point has been made: Because policy matters for families, it needs to be understood from a family perspective. This chapter will summarize definitions, historical developments, institutional characteristics, and policy and family frameworks relevant to family policy, and make some concluding observations and comments.

Family Policy: Domain, Definitions and Concept

Whereas some have talked about the futility of family policy, this book speaks to its potential for drawing attention to the relationship between families and policy and the importance of having ways to understand their relationship. Just as policy and social policy are about values that underlie choices and cut across issues at all levels of government, family policy also is about values that underlie choices that cut across issues at all levels of government. Whereas policy in general focuses on fundamental problems of individuals in relation to society, and social policy on the problems of social aggregates in relation to society, family policy as a subcategory of social policy focuses on the problems of families in relation to society. Whereas policy in general is most concerned about efficiency and the maximization of benefits to costs, social policy is concerned about needs that the market cannot or does not satisfy for certain segments of the population. Reflected in the choices that underlie specific social welfare measures that the workplace and tax system supplement, the former through measures known as occupational welfare and the latter through measures known as fiscal welfare, social policy helps to determine the level of well-being of individuals and groups in the society. Many of these measures have explicit family objectives; others have implicit family objectives. All affect families directly or indirectly, intentionally or not. Family policy as a concept and perspective calls attention to the family dimensions of these provisions, incorporating family well-being as a value to be maximized in conjunction with values that pertain to all policy areas: equity, efficiency, freedom, equality of opportunity, adequacy, rights, social cohesion, compassion, and so forth. Thus family policy has relevance for all families as well as particular families, and because of the continuing nature of family relationships, for individual members as well. Policy choices into which family considerations are deliberately structured are known as explicit or manifest family policies, the case of the Mental Retardation Family Subsidy Program being an example; policy choices into which family considerations are not deliberately structured but affect families nonetheless are known as implicit or latent family policies, the case of cost containment policies in elder care being an example. That most family policies in the United States are implicit or latent rather than explicit or manifest has served to obscure their family dimensions.

Historical Development of Family Policy in the United States

While the absence of explicit family policy may have obscured recognition of the family dimensions of policy, cultural traditions of minimal government, private property, and individualism have obscured myriad connections that linked families, government, and the economy to each other. Such traditions, while not completely governing institutional relationships between families, government, and the economy, have governed perceptions and normative definitions as to their relationship to each other. Because traditions have defined families as private and outside the realm of government's influence and the market's business, historically, except for poor families, families per se have not been items that have appeared on the public agenda. Although it has not yet cleared the halls of Congress, parental leave legislation has cleared the floors of some state legislatures, evidencing changing perceptions relative to institutional relationships between families, government, and the economy.

Expanding government programs, increasing numbers of female-headed households and working mothers, and the shift from a manufacturing to a service economy are indicative of the dramatic changes occurring in these three institutions—the family, government, and the economy—and their relationship to each other during the 1960s and 1970s. Because they are at odds with the ways in which people were taught to think about these three institutions, such changes have been regarded with dismay and confusion. Competing interpretations and definitions as to their meanings have been as confusing as the changes themselves. Some, noting that families were exposed and often adversely affected by the untrammeled effects of policy in other areas, called for a comprehensive and coherent family policy to guide government choices in areas that affected families directly. While many agreed as to the need for such a policy, they disagreed as to its specifics, particularly with respect to "moral" and economic issues, and the role that government should play in these two spheres. Others opposed such a policy altogether, believing that it would lead to the imposition of standards on family behaviors that they perceived as antithetical to the spontaneity and idiosyncratic nature of family life. Some objected because they associate family policy with family dependency on government, while others complained of the impotence of policy in affecting family circumstances. Still others regarded family policy as little more than an exercise in futility, adding only confusion, not substance, to existing confusions over policy issues, and a potential source of heightened conflict in the clash of views about families and government and their relationship to each other.

It was within this unsettled context that the first White House Conference on Families was held in the United States in 1980 to focus attention on the problems of families, what government was doing to contribute to these problems, and what it could do to alleviate them. Despite or because of the sharply conflicting views that found expression in the conference forums, both the connections between families and government and the problems that families experienced in these connections were highlighted. Incremental improvements in their connections and symbolic measures to demonstrate government's interest in families were later replaced by the view that prevailed during most of the eighties, that "government should get off the backs of families." This view, which shaped the direction of family policy in the

United States during this period, translated into lower taxes, cuts in spending for social programs, and increased spending for the military. Its consequences have been an increase in poverty, homelessness, hunger for millions of American families, increased social and income inequality, and a tremendous budget deficit to boot—none of which are consistent with the family well-being standard of family policy, or the individual well-being standard of social policy, or equity, vertically or intergenerationally. Nor are they consistent with compassion or social cohesion as values to be maximized. If future developments conform to the social change framework outlined in Chapter 2, such outcomes could constitute the situation that sets off a new round of policy debates and mobilized activity concerning different perceptions as to government's role for ensuring some agreed-upon level of individual and family well-being, which rest upon the achievement of such values as equity, social cohesion, compassion, efficiency, freedom, equality of opportunity, rights, and so forth.

Family Policy From an Institutional Perspective

While the values and traditions underlying existing institutional arrangements may have delayed recognition of the connections between families and policy, the structural characteristics of government in the United States preclude an orchestrated approach to family policy. Such characteristics include the system of checks and balances represented by the three branches of government, the executive, legislative, and judicial; the committee structure in Congress, which tends to reflect special, not overall or general family interests; the functional organization of government's administrative apparatus or agencies, such as health, education, welfare, and so forth; and the decentralization of power from the federal to state and local levels of government where the same situation prevails. Thus those who worry about the dangers of a comprehensive national family policy should take heart, given the structural characteristics of American government. Further, even when structures are created within governments, state or federal, in recognition of the connections between family and government, most are not meant to coordinate the actions of government in relation to families. Nor is it obvious at the state level that such structures make a difference in the legislative actions of state governments in relation to families, institutional factors related to federal-state relationships perhaps serving to minimize their effects, as in the case of child abuse legislation. Interorganizational networks such as the Council of State Governments and the National Association of Governors, which facilitate the exchange of information among members, also may minimize such effects.

Policy Frameworks for Understanding Family Policy

In addition to institutional factors that shape policies related to families, family policy also may reflect rational and deliberate assessments of alternative strategies and their consequences for the achievement of desired value/goals and objectives, such as different ways of delivering health care to promote family well-being while attending to cost or efficiency concerns. Family policy also may reflect incremental choices/actions as correctives to actions and choices of the past; some may reflect the equilibrium reached in the struggle among competing interest groups, or the preferences of elites, or the best that can be achieved under conditions of little or no authority, as in game theory. The case of welfare reform represents all of these choice situations. That a family framework was not applied in the deliberations about welfare reform is obvious from statements of government officials and the conclusions that were drawn about the family effects of the income maintenance experiments. These are good illustrations of why a family perspective and framework are important for interpreting data as to the effects of policy on families and why economic analyses by themselves are insufficient.

Family Frameworks for Shaping and Assessing Policy Choices

That economic analyses by themselves are insufficient for interpreting data pertaining to policies and families does not mean that a family perspective and framework by themselves are sufficient for this purpose either. Rather, multiple perspectives are needed, among which a family perspective surely is one. That more than one family framework also is needed was illustrated in the analysis of state-level public policy and individual and family well-being from a family systems perspective, which incorporated the concept of reciprocity from exchange theory. Thus, while the systems framework is the most comprehensive in terms of the concepts it provides for thinking about the relationship between families and government, concepts from other frameworks may still be needed to enhance analysis. In a similar fashion, the family systems perspective augmented the family stress framework in the analysis of the effects of alternative strategies to out-of-home care for mentally handicapped children and disabled elderly family members, suggesting that policy measures affecting one member affect all members of that system. In this regard, it is interesting to compare attitudes toward income provisions such as the alternative care grant and the family subsidy, which enable families to care for dependent members at home, with attitudes toward AFDC that enable low-income, female-headed families to do the same thing, the former regarded as cost saving, the latter as costly. Further, if the alternative care grant and family subsidy, both income assistance programs just as AFDC is, help families in stressful situations to balance the demands of their situation and thus meet them, the question may be asked as to why the same reasoning would not apply to AFDC as well.

Although conflict theory was not applied to any of the case examples of family policy, this was only because of the limitations of the illustrative data, not because it is not applicable. As earlier discussion noted, a feminist perspective certainly would have heightened the conflict created by the caregiving situation for mothers, wives, and daughters, and the gender bias underlying policy choices uncovered in the analysis of state public welfare and education expenditures in relation to state teen birthrates. The same comments might be said with respect to symbolic interaction as a frame of reference for thinking about the meanings of intersystem exchanges and transactions as they are experienced by families and members in a variety of situations.

The Case for the Application of Family Frameworks

While policy analysts and cost-conscious legislators may not be predisposed to apply family frameworks to the analysis of policy alternatives and their consequences out of the misguided notion that such frameworks are not relevant for policy choice, it is hoped that the findings reported in the three illustrative chapters will persuade them otherwise. That economic analysis is unable to calculate the costs of help not provided and services not rendered does not mean that such nonprovision is cost free, as exchange theory in fact advises and the analysis of state suicide rates and teen birthrates showed. While the family perspective that family policy offers draws attention to the family dimensions of such policy choices, the family frameworks give meaning to them, just as they give meaning to demographic data and trends about family structures and life. In this respect, they are a protection against the misinterpretation and misrepresentation of data pertaining to the effects of policies on families and counterproductive responding actions. In addition, they provide concepts for operationalizing the family well-being standard of family policy and for directing attention to policy areas or issues pertaining to families that require examination.

None of this is to suggest that other perspectives or analyses should not be applied to family policy issues. Rather, this book argues for multiple perspectives, of which the family surely is one, and the application of a family framework when the family dimensions of policy alternatives and their consequences are being assessed. The understandings derived from such application can then be incorporated into processes of choice so that whether these reflect rational or incremental choice processes, interest group equilibrium, elite preferences, or strategies employed under conditions of limited authority the choices that are made will at least be informed as to their implications for families and their members. In that families, for good or for ill, are such an important part of everyone's reality and perform so many critical functions for the larger society, the role that policy plays in their well- or ill-being warrants the same kind of time, attention, and understanding as the role that it plays in the workings of the economy and vice versa.

The Case for Understanding Family Policy

The questions raised about family policy, its connotation of family dependency on government, its potential dangers for family privacy and autonomy, the conceptual confusions it creates, and its potential for heightening conflict should not be dismissed cavalierly, even if they appear ill-founded. With regard to family dependency, families *are* dependent on government, just as government is dependent on families, both practically and conceptually, whether their relationship is viewed within the context of family policy or not. Thus the problem is not with the term or concept of family policy but the failure to recognize that families and government as interacting social systems within one another's environments are dependent on each other—inherently—in the very nature of their systemic needs and processes. With regard to the potential dangers of family policy for family privacy and the imposition of standards on family behaviors, such standards in fact already exist—with respect to the protection of family members from abuse, mandatory school attendance for children, the reporting of income for social security and income tax purposes, and to a host of other family matters—although not framed within the context of family policy. With respect to the conceptual confusions that family policy presumably creates, such confusions may be a function of its phase of conceptual development in that had the family dimensions of governmental policies been recognized much earlier, they would have been incorporated into existing ways of thinking about the relationship between families and government sooner. The trade-off between such temporary confusions and traditional ways of thinking about the relationship between families and government is continued inattention to the ways in which policies affect families, to the role that policy plays in shaping the worlds that families in different circumstances experience and in shaping the experience of males and females as family members, and to the stake that different interest groups and elites have in certain policy outcomes relative to families. In terms of heightened conflict, it is hard to understand how family policy as concept, perspective, field, or area of study, research, and practice, would heighten conflict that already exists over a range of family policy issues about which people already evidence strong differences, even when family policy is not the context in which such issues are framed. Nor is it reasonable in an area of social life as meaningful as the family to expect otherwise. In this regard, however, family policy is no different from other areas of policy in which emotions run high. The trick is to manage the conflict, not necessarily avoid it.

No attempt was made in any of this discussion to define families, taking a leaf from one critic who complained that the time spent in trying to arrive at common definitions might have been better spent in trying to deal with the issues. In my opinion, any ongoing social arrangement in which persons are committed to and care about each other, which meets their psychological, social, and physical needs, constitutes a family—or a friendship group, which, it is hoped, families are, too. Given the ongoing nature of family relationships, members may or may not share the same household any more than friends do. Although in general families connote roles such as mother and father, husband and wife, parents and children and siblings, it should be recognized that family relationships extend beyond these to include grandparents, aunts, uncles, cousins—and friends.

Conclusion

Thus the struggle over family policy is not just the struggle about traditional versus nontraditional views of family life or the policies that would promote one or the other. It also is a struggle between those who believe policy matters for families and those indifferent to the fact it does. Nor is the issue whether the United States should or should not have a national family policy; rather, the issue is how to think about policy in relation to families and whether and to what extent individual policies meet the standard of family well-being. Nor is the issue the futility of family policy but rather how policies can be shaped to promote family well-being, and the kinds of values and understandings they will reflect about families. It is within this context that family policy as concept, as perspective, as field, as area of study and research offers the greatest potential. To summarize:

(1) The United States does not have an overall comprehensive family policy, nor is it likely to have one.

(2) Nevertheless, all policy affects families directly or indirectly in both positive and negative ways.

(3) Therefore, in order to protect families from the unintended consequences of policies formulated for other purposes and to shape policies such that they meet the standard of family well-being, there is a need to understand policy in relation to families and families in relation to policy, and to influence its content and process accordingly.

Appendix

This section presents the major concepts for each of the frameworks presented in Chapters 1-6. The reader is advised to refer to the earlier chapters as aids to application.

Chapter 1
Family Policy: Definitions, Domain, and Concepts

Concepts/Definitions

- policy: important choices related to goal values of society
  - cluster of overall decisions
  - agreed-upon course of action
  - temporarily settled course of action
  - policy levels and scope: federal, regional, state, county, city, etc.
  - policy functions: distribute/redistribute, regulate, manage, promote
- social policy: all of the above
  - acts of government to meet range of needs market cannot or will not meet for certain populations
  - intervention in and regulation of an otherwise random social system
  - ideology underlying social welfare measures: income maintenance, health, housing, employment and human resources, social services, education
  - functions: compensation, social/personal investment, protection
  - fiscal and occupational welfare
- family policy: all of the above
  - implicit and explicit family goals and objectives

Orientation

- emphasis on problems of individuals in relation to society

- emphasis on individuals and social aggregates
- concerned with social consequences of policies in other areas, that is, social costs and externalities

- emphasis on families and consequences of policies for families

- manifest and latent family goals
  and objectives
- intended and unintended consequences of policies for
  families
- direct and indirect consequences of policies for families
- family well-being as a criterion
- a perspective and field of
  activity

- relevance for *all* families

Chapter 2
Developments in Family Policy:
Reflections of Social Change

Concepts and Basic Ideas

- value conflict and contradictions: individualism, private
  property/free market, minimum
  government, justice, equality,
  rights
- oscillation of prevailing value
  themes over time
- structural changes/novel situation:
  family, government, and economy

- competing definitions of novel
  situation
  - family disintegrating
  - government is too big, usurping
    family functions, drag on
    economy
  - policies contradictory; need
    explicit family policy to guide
    government actions affecting
    families
- mobilization/organization of
  activity around competing definitions of situation
- social action/any procedural,
  legislative, organizational reform
  - White House Conferences on
    Families

  - 1981 Omnibus Reconciliation
    Act: cutbacks on services and
    programs and tax cut

Assumptions

- inherent in institutional arrangements

- all values cannot be maximized
  at the same time
- selection of one value over
  another creates conflict within
  and between individuals and
  groups

- minimal government best

- absence of explicit family policy
  leads to policies and programs
  that have harmful unintended
  consequences for families

- creates conditions for next
  cycle of social change
- heightening of awareness of
  ways in which government affects
  families
- costs of government a drag on the
  economy and family budgets

- creation of congressional and
  state government committees
  to attend to family related issues
- increasing poverty and income
  disparities
- novel situation and competing definitions of situations: repetition of
  cycle

- need structure to support
  concern for families within
  government

Chapter 3
An Institutional Perspective
for Understanding Family Policy

Concepts and Basic Ideas

- institutions: patterns of activity
  governed by norms, values; persist
  over time; roles, patterns of
  behavior, structures and structural
  arrangements
- policy: outcome of government
  processes and structures; distinguished by its legitimacy, authority, and universality
- Constitution as body of rules

Assumptions

- norms governing institutional
  arrangements favor some outcomes and prevent others, such as
  a coherent policy approach to
  families

- all persons are created equal, have
  certain inalienable rights; government derives its power from the
  consent of the people, and is prevented from violating its power by
  system of checks and balances and
  rules that govern institutional
  arrangements

Chapter 4
Policy Frameworks for Understanding Family Policy

THE RATIONAL CHOICE FRAMEWORK:
POLICY AS RATIONAL CHOICE

Concepts

- Goals and objectives
- Alternative goals and objectives
- Consequences of goals and
  objectives

Assumptions

- Any action reflects combination of
  relevant values and objectives, perceived alternatives, estimates of
  consequences, and net valuation

- Consequences of alternatives
- Choice based on net value achievement
- Efficiency: ratio between valued inputs and outputs

- Assumes all relevant values known and that in any course of action, sacrifice of some values will be compensated by attainment of others

INCREMENTAL POLICY FRAMEWORK: POLICY AS INCREMENTAL CHOICE

Concepts	*Assumptions*
• Existing policy as variations of past	• Existing programs structure situations of choice
• Policies and programs as outputs	• Problems too complex to understand comprehensively
• Uncertainty and uncertainty avoidance	• Departures from existing policies involve unknown risks
• Satisficing	• Find good enough course of action
• Political feasibility	• Reliance on prompt corrective
• Bounded rationality	emphasizing short run feedback
• Goals as emergent rather than predetermined	rather than accurate predictions of future
• Sequential attention to goals	

GAME APPROACH TO POLICY: POLICY AS RATIONAL CHOICE UNDER COMPETITIVE CONDITIONS

Concepts	*Assumptions*
• policy is outcome of the game; choice under competitive conditions	• policymaking situations are games involving interdependent moves of relevant players
• strategy; tactics; minimax	• outcomes depend on choices and actions of two or more players
• competition; influence, power	• interdependent moves reflect desires and abilities of individual players and their expectations of other's choices
	• rules of game define choices available to players
• negotiation and negotiating skill; persuasion, accommodation	
• bargaining; compromises; payoffs; stakes of the game	• game is played under conditions of no authority
• actors as players in positions	• interests of government leaders are competitive, shaped by positions within structure that shape their attitudes and perceptions

- uncertainty and uncertainty avoidance

- policy is process of conflict and consensus building; competition for support requires use of persuasion, accommodation, and bargaining

INTEREST GROUP FRAMEWORK: POLICY CHOICE AS EQUILIBRIUM IN STRUGGLE BETWEEN INTEREST GROUPS

Concepts	*Assumptions*
• group demands; group becomes political when attempts to exert influence on government	• groups rather than individuals compete for influence on government
• the group: individuals organized around shared interests and attitudes	• task of political system is to manage group conflict
• group conflict and compromise; negotiation and bargaining	
• policy as equilibrium reached among contending groups	• changes in group influence can be expected to be reflected in public policy, which shifts toward groups gaining influence and away from those losing it
• group influence: wealth, size, cohesion, leadership, access to decision makers	
• coalitions	• coalition of groups for mobilizing and channeling efforts to achieve goal

ELITE THEORY: POLICY CHOICE AS ELITE PREFERENCES

Concepts	*Assumptions*
• power	• groups rank higher or lower on some critical dimension; hierarchical ranking of groups gives rise to elitism
• manipulation	
• bargaining	
• persuasion	• public policy reflects values and interests of elites
• fixed elites	• fixed power; manipulation of conditions and institutional arrangements to favor elites; same group exercises power even though issues change
• revolving elites	• fluid power; pluralistic model using bargaining and negotiation and face-to-face interactions

- governing elites

- strategic elites

- size and complexity of society precludes everyone's participation; some division of labor is required
- because of its strategic position in society, able to determine framework for discussion of policy alternatives
- group competition over narrow range of issues

Chapter 5
Families as Social Systems:
Implications for Family Policy

Concepts	*Assumptions*
• system functions: family	• all systems have tasks to perform to meet needs of members and environment
• physical care of family members	
• membership: procreation/ adoption/relinquishment	
• socialization of members	
• social control of members	
• production/consumption	
• moral and motivation of members	
• interdependence of system parts/ positions	• certain roles must be performed if system is to perform its functions
• family: husband-wife, brother-sister, father-son, father-daughter, mother-son, mother-daughter, etc.	
	• family relational network continues until behaviors of member disrupt it; varies with social class and culture
• structural deficit	• tasks of unoccupied positions must be reallocated to others, resulting in the overburdening of existing positions
• structural excess	• too many occupants for given positions may result in competition and conflict
• boundary maintenance	• boundaries help to separate systems from each other and from their environment
• liaison roles	
• linkage competence	• family as system more closed/ private than other systems

- system equilibrium and adaptation tendencies

- feedback and information from environment

- negative feedback

- positive feedback

- mapping for variety

- environment: general/specific; dynamic, complex, and interactive, that is, turbulent

- assumes range of states within which systems can function
- family vulnerable to disequilibrium internally induced because of variable size and changing age composition and externally induced by environment
- used to guide system functioning; feedback incongruent with system goals basis for modifying system behaviors and operations
- oriented toward status quo or homeostasis, bringing divergent system behaviors into convergence with system values
- oriented toward change or morphogenesis; deviation amplifying rather than reducing
- systems need continuous flow of varied information, experience, and input from environment to meet changing needs of members and environment
- increasingly, environmental conditions present systems with sudden unpredictable changes that threaten their equilibrium and adaptive capacities

NOTE: System concepts may be applied to government at all levels, looking at policy as system outputs.

Chapter 6
Other Family Frameworks and
Their Implications for Family Policy

EXCHANGE AND CHOICE THEORIES

Concepts

- rewards: pleasures, satisfactions, gratifications from statuses, relationships
- costs: unpleasant relationships, interactions, situations, statuses, feelings, forgone rewards resulting

Assumptions

- humans are rational; seek to maximize rewarding behaviors and avoid costly ones within limits of information and ability to predict future

from choosing competing alternatives
- profitable relationships/
experiences
- comparison level

- comparison level alternatives

- reciprocity: interdependence,
mutuality

- people seek profitable relationships
- people compare their situations
with those of others and evaluate
them accordingly
- potential for profitable outcome
must compensate and absorb
costs of moving out of old and
into new situation
- people should help, not hurt,
those who help them, superseding
the principle of profitability

CONFLICT THEORY

Concepts	*Assumptions*
- competition - cooperation - compromise	- conditions of scarcity create competitive zero-sum structure; gains for one create losses for others - situations structured such that individuals can win at expense of others or all can win or lose as a group - rules necessary when conflicting interests at stake
- negotiation - bargaining - aggression - power/authority; ability to control situation - privilege: competitive advantage related to position or access to scarce resources - promises and threats	- negotiation, bargaining: attempts to influence direction of contested events or decisions - rely on shared meanings

SYMBOLIC INTERACTION

Concepts	*Assumptions*
- socialization: acquisition by person of values, norms, attitudes of social groups to which he/she belongs - anticipatory socialization	- developmental/over time - focus on normal as opposed to pathological behaviors - people live in a symbolic as well as physical environment; symbols may be auditory, linguistic, visual; meanings are cultural

- role: behavior, performance, enactment, interpersonal competence
- role: expectations, dissensus and consensus, involvement, ambiguity, location, compatibility/congruence, rewards, strains, and accumulation
- definition of situation

- satisfaction: congruence between expectations and rewards
- relative deprivation

- roles dynamic, emerge through social interaction

- acquired through social interactions and development of repertoire of role skills

- definition of situation influences its effects such that the latter tends to be congruent with the definition

FAMILY STRESS THEORY

Concepts

- stressor event: normative/non-normative
- family definition of situation

- family resources

- family capacity or incapacity for meeting demands of situation, the latter being a potential crisis

- additional stressors, or stress pile-up
- additional resources
- modifications in family perceptions of situation
- family coping strategies

Assumptions

- stressor events involve changes in family interaction, goals, boundaries, or demands that family is required to meet
- depending on family's resources, and appropriateness for the situation, demands have potential for upsetting balance needed for effective family functioning
- whether situation becomes a crisis depends on family's evaluation and definition of it and their resources for meeting demands of situation
- families seldom deal with a single stressor

- families change over time; nature of demands they experience changes accordingly
- new resources may become available to families
- may redefine situation in light of changes

Index

About the Author

SHIRLEY L. ZIMMERMAN is Professor of Family Social Science at the University of Minnesota, where she teaches family policy, family policy research, and comparative family policy. She has served as consultant to numerous state and local social agencies in planning and developing educational programs for professional staff and in the conduct of research. Her own research in recent years has focused on the relationship between families and public policies as reflected in such programs as adult day care for elderly disabled family members, the family subsidy program for families with mentally handicapped children, and in state expenditures for public welfare, education, and health. She is the author of many articles that focus on the effects of public policies on families in different life circumstances. She is a former NIMH Fellow in the Family Impact Analysis Training Program, sponsored by the Family Study Center at the University of Minnesota in the late 1970s.

NOTES

NOTES

NOTES